LIFE AND SAYINGS OF MOTHER YOANA

SAINT **SHENOUDA** PRESS

Life and Sayings of Mother Yoana

ST SHENOUDA PRESS
SYDNEY, AUSTRALIA
2024

ST SHENOUDA PRESS
8419 Putty Rd,
Putty, NSW, 2330
Sydney, Australia

www.stshenoudapress.com

ISBN 13: 978-0-6457704-4-5

Cover Design:
Hani Ghaly,
Begoury Graphics
begourygraphics@gmail.com

Contents

Preface

"I will bless you...and you shall be a blessing." (Gen 12:2)

We saw with our own eyes and we touched with our own hands the reality of this promise in the life of our mother, the beloved Tamav Yoana, the head of the monastery of nuns.

The Lord blessed her life and her struggle and she yielded many fruits. Her life was a sweet smelling aroma and a song that reached up to heaven and made the Lord's heart joyful, along with His angels and saints.

Truly, her life was a symbol and a teaching: a symbol of strong spiritual work and a teaching for those who live the life of monasticism. She was a living example, teaching us how to live and gain the fruit of the spirit.

"But the fruit of the Spirit is love, joy, peace, longsuffering, kindness, goodness, faithfulness, gentleness, self-control." (Gal 5:22-23)

Whoever knew our beloved mother Tamav Yoana experienced the sweetness, beauty and growth of her fruitful life. The grace of God made her joyful appearance and gentle smile encouraging to many souls. Just by seeing her, their relationship became stronger with God and they had the power to repent.

Truly, the Lord has blessed you, Tamav Yoana, and you became blessed. You became a blessed mother for this generation and for our monastery. The place is blessed because of you and sacred because of your prayers and chastity. We need you to lift up your heart unto the Lord because He will never refuse you. We are your daughters living through your blessings.

"The righteous man walks in his integrity; His children are blessed after him." (Proverbs 20:7)

My beloved mother, how can only several pages hold all your life? Your relationship with God was strong. How can our weak souls perceive this?

+++

Our beloved mother, we were interrupted many times in preparing this book and what we illustrate is only a few drops in the ocean of your virtues. Excuse our weakness. May the Lord open our eyes so we can become like you.

Our pure mother Tamav Yoana, we celebrate your wedding. The wedding of the victorious bride to her heavenly groom. Enjoy the paradise ceremony, where there is no agony or fear. Remember us, as we are your children. Ask the Lord to assist us.

Let us hold firm to what we have learned from you and continue to fight in God's way in peace. Soon we will see you in the presence of our kind God and our heart will rejoice with the Angels when we hear your meek voice saying to our Holy God:

"Here I am and the children whom the Lord has given me!" (Isaiah 8:18)

Our beloved mother, you had a very special place in the heart of H.H Pope Shenouda. You learnt from his monastic knowledge as he was your confession father while you were in the house of consecration in Giza. He attended your funeral and prayed on your purified body. He was so emotional yet he stayed up to comfort the sad hearts of all your daughters. Truly, his fatherhood and the spring of his love affected our souls and soothed us with heavenly comfort.

From our deepest hearts, we thank our gentle father for we saw sincere love come out of a kind heart. We learned from Him how to be truly loyal.

May our good Lord protect His life for so many years in peace with the intercession of the Mother of God, the Virgin Saint Mary and the prayers of the Prince of martyrs St George, our monasteries Patron.

Your daughters,
The Nuns of Saint George Monastery
Old Cairo
1st May 2000
The Feast of Prince of Martyrs
Great Saint George

Chapter 1

Her Childhood

Her Childhood

Recorded by Mr Morris Mosaad (Tamav Yoana's brother)

"Before I formed you in the womb I knew you; Before you were born I sanctified you." (Jeremiah 1:5)

Tamav Yoana was born to a simple family. Her father was from Nakhila (Markaz Abu Teeg) in the Council of Assiut. He lived in Giza and worked in a garden field in the ministry of agriculture. Her mother was a housewife.

This family faced a hard tribulation. The mother was barren for many years and when she did give birth, the child would die straight after. The mother continually prayed to Saint Mary until one day she saw Saint Mary in a dream. St Mary gave her two cents and a paper money in her hands. (The two cents symbolised two boys, while the paper money symbolised a girl that would be blessed.)

The boy grew up well and reached childhood. Whenever he fell sick, the mother would fear because all her previous children had passed away after birth. This boy is named Mr Morris Saad and became a manager of the central Bank.

For 7 full years, the mother had several other children yet all passed away very early in age. However, on the 26th of August 1941, she had a daughter called Blanche. The word "Blanche" means "white" and resembled the pure life she would live. Blanche's brother, Saed, also survived. Blanche was very close to her brother. She looked after him as a teacher and friend.

The Lord allowed our beloved Tamav Yoana to live her childhood in a school of tribulation. This prepared her for the strong responsibilities that would later come in her life. Similarly, the Lord used many tribulations to train many of the great saints of our church like our mother the virgin Saint Mary, Moses the prophet, the righteous Joseph and David the prophet.

"It is good for a man to bear the yoke in his youth." (Jeremiah 3:27)

Blanche and her brothers lived an unhappy life, as her father was always harsh and busy with work. They never experienced love and care from their father. In addition, the mother had lost many previous children so she feared for them so much. As a result, they were prevented from leaving the house, playing or even going excursions.

One day when Blanche was sick, her mother decided to take her to visit the old churches in Old Cairo. Her mother entered the cell of St George in Saint George Monastery for women and took the blessings of the Chain in his cell. A nun carried Blanche to the icon of St George. After taking the blessing of the icon, Blanche became healed instantly. Since that time, she never felt sick during her childhood.

"He who protects the children is our Lord." (Psalm 114:6)

One of the nuns who was a Sunday school servant in St Mark church in Giza said, "One day I was surprised to see a young girl for the first time sitting in the first row of a year 1 class. She was only 10 years old, yet she was concentrating and very keen to understand the lesson.

After the lesson finished, I introduced myself to her and I found that her dad usually prevented her from coming and attending the class. I went to her house and I asked her dad to allow her to attend since she was a very talented girl and loved by everyone. With the love of God, her father allowed her to go to church and we became very close friends."

Throughout her childhood and youth, Blanche had to endure the emotional state of her mother who always feared any danger happening to her since she had lost so many previous children. She also had to endure the harsh attitudes of her father.

Her brother, Mr Morris, states that despite her difficult childhood, Blanche never rebelled, got depressed or became defiant to any orders. Instead, she accepted everything that was given to her.

She was always top in her studies and achieved the highest HSC mark in the country. The country celebrated and honoured her with awards and gifts consisting of literature books. However, she was very sad when her father refused her entry into university. This may have been due to the large expenses required. She ended up working as a teacher in Manyal, Cairo. She was always honest and hard working.

Mrs Soufie Youssef (one of the teachers) said: "When I was a supervisor 38 years ago, I always admired this little quiet teacher. Her work was always great. She knew how to prepare good activities and deliver the material to her kids. We never had a teacher like her."

Also Mrs Ansaaf Saeed, a colleague teacher with Tamav, said: "Miss Blanche was a truly great teacher. She always had great virtues that made her different to everyone else. All her colleagues at school witnessed that.

She was always an example of love, humbleness, obedience and quietness. These were all qualities in her life. She was loved by all, lived in peace, was never ill tempered, loved everyone, was kind, gentle and served with integrity. She taught her children with great honesty and ensured that the information was delivered well. She never rejected anybody and never refused any work."

Blanche loved solitary; she enjoyed spiritual reading, praying her Psalms and her normal prayers. She never mixed with people unless she had to. She was very different to everyone else, yet she was filled with grace.

After she finished her day at school, she would usually meet with Mother Irini Daoud, a nun from St Marys Monastery for women in Haret Zeweilah, Cairo. This nun taught her Tasbeha (praises), after which she would head home.

Mr Morris said, "She was never interested in materialistic things such as her beauty, make up, her hair or even going to a hairdresser. Her smiley and happy face was seen by all that saw her."

Chapter 2

Her Service In Sunday School

Blanche loved Father Salib Sorial, the priest of St Mark church in Guiza Cairo. She always sought his help and guidance.

She grew in righteousness and started to serve in Sunday school while still in high school. She was the youngest servant there. Father Salib trusted her a lot so he gave her the responsibility of Youth meeting too. Blanche's heart was full of love and sacrifice.

Father Salib loved Blanche very much that he got his eldest daughter to be in her Sunday school class.

"From childhood you have known the Holy Scriptures, which are able to make you wise for salvation through faith which is in Christ Jesus." (2 Tim 3:15)

Zakia Moawad was also a servant in Blanche's Sunday School class and she said, "Miss Blanche always lived the life of prayers. She always prayed before and after meals, before she took me for visitation services and before we entered in the house of a person to visit. She taught me how to pray in every occasion. We used to pray "Our Father" together as she dropped me home. She always reminded me of this verse: "And those who seek me diligently will find me." (proverbs 8:17)

She always advised us to come to church early. She taught us humility and showed us the right way to dress and cover our body. She was always very simple in her clothing: long sleeve blouse with small collar and a pleat skirt with soft colour. She always wore long stockings and black shoes, even in summer. She never carried a bag but only her small bible. She always said, "Carry neither money bag, knapsack." (Luke 10:4)

From her service in Sunday school, she had a special place in our hearts. She used to give us spiritual exercises to follow throughout the week. She used to write notes in our exercise book with her own handwriting. She would pass an aluminium box and encourage us to give tithes. Then, we would empty this box and use the money to buy gifts for those in need. She would also distribute rice, sugar, pasta and chocolate to the poor. She used to take us to visit a solitude nun who lived in an isolated room, beside the church. She would also take us to visit the sick in hospital, the orphans and the blind who used to live near a station street.

During the afternoon, we would visit widowers. Blanche would take her Bible, read for them and comfort them. We learned so much from her. She was truly chosen and gifted by God since her childhood."

+++

Dr Neebal Morcos, a dentist, knew Blanche since high school. She said: "Blanche was tidy, punctual in her time and very intelligent in her study. God was with her in whatever she did, as He was with Joseph the righteous. She was always serious in her work. We all loved her, respected her presence and never joked in front of her. If we did joke, she would change the speech into a more beneficial one. During recess at school, she talked about God and His Saints. I never saw her eating at recess as she was fasting.

During an excursion to Luxor and Aswan, she was with us and always kept silent although all the girls laughed with loud voices. At night, we would all sleep but she would stay up with her Agpia and pray.

She inspired me to attend Sunday school in Guiza and to get to know the late Reverend Father Saleeb Sorial. Blanche became our guide and spiritual soldier."

Chapter 3

Her Desire For Consecration

Blanche had the love of God in her life and in her heart. She loved to consecrate her life for the heavenly groom. She refused all marital ideas.

The Father priest Salib Sorial offered her marriage to a priest to be, but she refused.

She had a very strong relationship with her Sunday School Servant who became the co-ordinator in service. This servant always took her to visit monasterys and to attend Bible study. She allowed Blanche to teach Bible Study to a Christian girls group because Blanche had a desire to do that.

This Sunday school coordinator soon became a nun. Tamav Kereya invited Blanche to come attend the ceremony because she knew of Blanche's close relationship to this Sunday school teacher.

Tamav Kereya used to give Blanche the key of her own cell so she could rest during the midnight prayers. Consequently, this cell became the cell of Tamav Yoana when she later became the head nun of St George Monastery.

Joining the monastery

Mr Morris said, "One day, my father surprisingly found a letter in the house, written by Blanche. In this letter, she wrote that she had chosen the way of monasticism and had entered the St George monastery in old Cairo. This surprised the entire family.

As soon as my father read the letter, he came quickly to my house to take me to the late pope Kyrillos VI. We went to see his Holiness and my father explained to him what had happened. He asked the Pope to send Blanche back home, as he could not live without her. The pope told him to go to the monastery and tell the nuns that Blanche was not going to go in the way of monasticism this time.

When we arrived at the monastery, Blanche refused to come with us. My father grabbed her firmly and tried very aggressively to make her return. Blanche fell on the stairs of the monastery, but thanks to God, she did not get hurt.

Eventually, we forced her out of the monastery and I took her to my flat. She closed the door of the room on herself and spend the whole time crying bitterly. She refused food and drink all day.

After my father calmed down, Blanche returned to her father's house and lived in an isolated room.

The late father reverend Salib Sorial went to his holiness Pope Kyrillos and inquired him about what had happened. The pope told him not to be upset as she would return back to the monastery. Pope Kyrillos' words were true as she later returned to St George monastery and became a head nun."

Chapter 4

Joining the Consecrated House

Blanche found it difficult to join the monastery and consecrate herself to the Lord due to her father's demands. Eventually Fr Saleeb Sorial persuaded Blanche's father to let her join the Consecrated House of St Demiana.

She joined the Consecrated House and showed much love to all sisters. As documented by the late Miss Jasmine, there were two houses for consecration: one partial consecration House and one full consecration house. Tamav Yoana joined the full consecration House.

Tamav Yoana loved the Paradise of the Fathers; She read this book everyday as she wanted to follow everything that was written in it. She became an actual doer of the words. One virtue that she possessed was LOVE. Her love was so amazing.

There are many incidents that prove her practical love and sacrifice:

1)   One of the nuns say: "I had a gown that was very old and torn so I washed and hanged it on the clothes line to dry. When I went to get it from the clothes line, I found that my old gown had a new collar and new buttons sewed. Therefore, I hesitated to take it because it could not be mine. I asked one of the sisters if this gown belonged to me and the sister said "yes." I asked her who had fixed my gown but she did not know. The next day, I saw small material pieces in Miss Blanche's room. From that, I knew that she was the one who fixed my gown."

2)   When Pope Shenouda was a Bishop, he was the confession father of this Consecrated House. He prepared a specific daily program which included some rest time in the middle of the day. In her rest time, Tamav Yoana would continue with her works,

which confirmed her love.

In this house of consecration, everyone was responsible for the kitchen on a certain week. During one week, one of the nuns was responsible for cleaning all the rice and beans from any dirt. When she went to do her job, she found the rice was already clean. She was surprised and when she asked who cleaned it, nobody answered. The next day, it was discovered that Blanche had cleaned the rice during her rest time, although this task was not even on her rostered duty week.

Another time it was noticed that she put the best food for others and left the less quality food for herself.

When the nuns would bring her new winter clothes to wear, she would start crying. Several times, the nuns asked her why she was crying. Tamav Yoana would say that in the Paradise of the Fathers, a monk doesn't wear new clothes. She completely refused to wear the clothes but finally wore them out of obedience.

+++

In one of Pope Shenouda's visitations, he stayed from morning to afternoon and he was delivering sermons. Blanche refused to sit down in his presence as she quoted from the Paradise of the Fathers, "Don't sit in the presence of the elders." She only sat down when she had been ordered by Pope Shenouda himself.

She loved to do the midnight praises (tasbeha) everyday and she asked Pope Shenouda for permission to do this. He told her to divide the tasbeha into sections for each night, but she would go into her room and pray the whole Tasbeha. She always loved prayers because she loved to stay with the Lord and live the life of prayer. She was doing more work than she should have, yet always with guidance.

She always lived isolated as she loved solitude. She never spoke even when she found two sisters talking together. She would walk softly beside them and enter in quietly to her room. If someone asked her to come and join, she would apologise in humility and say, "If I go in the middle of the conversation, I will make things worse." However, this was not true. If there was any conflict, she always faced it with heavenly wisdom.

She was always characterised with a low, soft, gentle voice. However in Sunday school, she explained the lesson with a loud and confident voice, ensuring that every student could hear her.

Blanch loved the Bible and studied it very deeply. In between each page would be a piece of paper on which she wrote all her thoughts and contemplations. Her contemplations were always deep and spiritually lifting.

"Blessed is the man who listens to me, Watching daily at my gates, Waiting at the posts of my doors. For whoever finds me, finds life, and obtains favour from the Lord." (Proverbs 8:34-35)

Truly, the consecrated heart is the heart that is circumcised with the Lord Jesus, an eternal circumcision announced as holy. A consecrated heart is always thankful, always wanting to talk about the Lord Jesus. A consecrated heart is full of joy, void of sadness, because the Lord is dwelling in it. A consecrated heart has all its ways set on the Lord, believes all things work for good. This was the heart of Miss Blanche.

Miss Blanche stayed in the house of consecration for a few years. She grew in the life of solitude and yielded virtues of monasticism with the guidance of her confession father, Pope Shenouda.

During this time, she used to visit the monastery of Abu Seifein and train under Tamav Irini, the head of the monastery.

At this point, her father was finally convinced and he allowed her to live inside Abu Seifen monastery.

"He has determined their pre-appointed times and the boundaries of their dwellings." (Acts 17: 26)

Chapter 5

Her Life in Abu Seifin Monastery

Written by the blessed mother, Tamav Irini
The head of Abu sefein Monastery for women

The life of Tamav Yoana was a flowing river of spirituality. Her life was blessed. She poured her monastic virtues at the Saviour's feet, either in secret or in public.

Blanche Mosaad Metri joined Abu Sefein monastery for women on the 9th of September 1969, after many battles from her father and members of her family.

From 9/9/1969 until 06/03/1971, everyone around the monastery had noticed her precise and serious attitude towards her spiritual life. Everyone noticed her obedience, her humility and her purity. The Lord bestowed on her great virtues.

With time, she grew in obedience and understanding of the monastery regulations. At the start of the 40 holy fasting days of 1971, the monastery was joyful as it was preparing for the coming of new nuns, who had just finished their period of trial.

At the dawn of 6th of March 1971, Pope Shenouda asked Fr Athanasios El Antony, the head of St Anthony Monastery and the confession father of the monastery for women at that time, to celebrate with the new nuns of the monastery.

The trial period for anyone who wants to join a monastery is usually 3 years. On that special day, they grabbed Blanche and ordained her a nun, although she had not finished her training period yet. Blanche was very surprised and astonished at the unexpected ordination. The whole congregation experienced deep joy for her. The celebration ended with tears of happiness, especially after the big surprise of Mother Yoana's ordination.

After she became a nun, her heart was filled with great humility and purity. Every day she grew and became strong in spirit with the presence of God in her life. She attained a high level of holiness. She always attended prayer meetings, tasbeha and liturgies. She never missed them unless she was very sick.

"Blessed are the pure in heart, for they shall see God." (Matthew 5:8)

Tamav Yoana's prayers were spontaneous. They were deep like a flame, reaching out to the Lord. She loved midnight praises and Psalms very much. Her meek soul was one of a child. She always prayed without ceasing. She never wasted her time but was always seen working, praying or meditating. She was always busy in her cell, following the rule: "From your work to your cell to your prayers. Keep these always and you will flee from the devils tricks."

She also loved hymns and spiritual songs as she sang them with depth, understanding and simplicity of heart.

Mother Yoana and her service with the congregation

Beside her duties in the monastery, she always looked after the sick people. She did so with great love. She used no differentiation and no comparison. She always served with humility and sacrificed herself to please everyone. She was always known as the "beloved mother" because her virtue of love was evident to all. She had a pleasant style of answering questions. Her answers were honest and simple. Her laughs and jokes were composed.

"God gives grace to the humble." (1Peter 5:5)

A Role model to her sister nuns and novices

The life of Mother Yoana was centred around obedience. This is a main foundation stone in the monastic life. During her spiritual trainings, whenever she was given a task, she would stick to it and reply with love and Joy. Her heart was always shining. It became a place of rest to many people, as well as the Holy Spirit, which filled her with understanding and spiritual depth. Whenever she was praised, she shone in humility and self-denial.

Gathering for Bible commentary

She had the responsibility of explaining the Holy Bible to others. With all gentleness and humility, she researched and read the Bible precisely. Words full of grace were always on her lips. Her contemplations were deep and holy.

"The secret of the Lord is with those who fear Him, And He will show them His covenant." (Psalm 25:14)

"But God has revealed them to us through His Spirit. For the Spirit searches all things, yes, the deep things of God." (1Cor 2:10)

She was highly gifted in meditating on the Holy Books and offering explanations. Her explanations were very clear and simple.

She was always growing in grace, humility and holiness.

Tamav Yoana and her responsibility for the security of the monastery.

When the monastery first brought new land in Alexandria, the mother superior had to travel to complete some duties. During this time, she would leave the responsibility of the monastery for Tamav Yoana due to her honesty, love and pious commitment.

Tamav Yoana was filled with grace. Her light shined before all people as she was always held in the hand of God.

"No one, when he has lit a lamp, puts it in a secret place or under a basket, but on a lamp stand that it may give light to all who are in the house." (Luke 11:33)

Mother Yoana's ordination as Mother Superior over St George Monastery, Old Cairo 11/09/1980

Tamav Kereya, head of St George monastery passed away on the 13th August 1980. Pope Shenouda asked Tamav Irini (the head of Abu Sefein monastery) to be responsible for this monastery until a replacement was found. During this period, Tamav Irini would visit the monastery every day and take with her one of her nuns. One day Mother Yoana was the one to go with Tamav Irini.

When they arrived, Mother Yoana felt a very strange feeling. She felt a warm motherhood feeling towards all the nuns. She confessed this feeling to her confession father who was at that time Late Reverend Angelos El Sourani. He calmed her saying: "If this is from God, let it be." The Lord was actually preparing her heart for this responsibility.

When Pope Shenouda arrived to St George Monastery for women in Old Cairo, he took the opinion of all the nuns there as to who should be their next Mother Superior. All the nuns elected one from St Abu Sefein monastery.

Pope Shenouda asked Tamav Irini to choose a girl from her monastery who would fit this responsibility. Tamav Irini prayed and asked the Lord for guidance. Every time Tamav Irini thought of this topic, Mother Yoana always came to her mind. Tamav Irini wanted to keep Mother Yoana in her monastery but God kept exposing His will, in that Mother Yoana was to be the head of St George monastery.

Later on, Tamav Irini announced to all the nuns in St Abu Sefein monastery that Mother Yoana would become the mother superior of St George monastery. When Mother Yoana heard the news, she cried severely because she felt her weakness and the weight of this great responsibility. All the nuns cried with her. Tamav Irini calmed her down with her motherhood and wisdom. She talked to her about the power of God and how His strength is made perfect in our weakness. Mother Yoana accepted the will of God and took on the responsibility. St Abu Sefein monastery joyfully offered a great and expensive jewel to the monastery of St George.

The late head of St George monastery, Tamav Kereya, saw a vision that mother Yoana will be the head of the monastery after her departure. So when Tamav Kereya was visiting St Abu Sefein monastery, she sat beside the door of the monastery and told Mother Yoana : "Give me the key to the door and I will look after it while you go to St George monastery and take responsibility over me." Tamav Yoana cut her off with gentleness as she was astonished by these words.

The blessed mother Yoana was ordained on Thursday 11th of September 1980 (day of El Nayrouz) by the hand of His holiness Pope Shenouda the Third, in the presence of Bishop Mettaos.

Tamav Irini, the Abbotess of St Abu Sefein was present in the celebration with lots of nuns from her monastery. Blessed Mother Mariam, the Abbotess of St Mary monastery in Haret Zeweila and the Late Tamav Aghabi, Abbotess of St George monastery in Haret Zweila, were also present. Tamav Yoana was the first one ordained by Pope Shenouda. There were special prayers in celebration of this occasion. Tamav Yoana started a new road of strive. She carried the burden, looking up to Jesus, her one goal.

At that time, there were 22 nuns. Some feared her because they did not know her, but soon they saw her true motherhood and began to love Tamav Yoana. She was not merely an abbess, but a close sister to all the nuns. "Be a son in between your brotherhood and be a brother in between your kids."

After one year of her ordination, Tamav Yoana started accepting more girls into monasticism. She taught them the way of monasticism and its rules. The monastery became a paradise on earth for all the nuns. Tamav was always working hard, becoming a role model in everything she did.

" In all things showing yourself to be a pattern of good works; in doctrine showing integrity, reverence, incorruptibility." (Titus 2: 7)

Mother Yoana would gather all the nuns to pray the third hour of the Agpia. This prayer was for the peace of all churches, for whoever was in tribulation and for those who asked to be remembered in prayer. She also gathered the nuns at sunset, giving them a spiritual sermon.

At midnight, she used to ring the bell and gather all the nuns for the midnight prayer. She attended the midnight prayer up until her departure, even during her periods of sickness.

She loved hymns and the Lord gifted her with a strong angelic voice. She always sung the tunes with a spirit of prayer. This comforted any person who listened to her sing. Tamav taught all the hymns and tunes to her fellow nuns and made sure that everyone knew them.

She attended masses and vespers. As she entered the church, she would bow in reverent three times before the Lord.

When she stood for prayer, she would stand very respectfully. She would never lean on anything although she suffered spine pain and the doctors told her not to stand much.

She organised for all the nuns to gather on one table for food. Paradise of Monks would be read while they were eating. She utilised Anba Pachomius' system which involved communal life and service between all the nuns.

"And had all things in common." (Acts 2: 44)

Whenever the bell would ring, signally that food was to be prepared; Tamav Yoana would rush straight away and help with this task. She supported the nuns and the beginners in everything and she was always there for them. She joined them in everything. She was a role model and a silent example.

"Yes, you yourselves know that these hands have provided for my necessities, and for those who were with me." (Acts 20:34)

Tamav Yoana taught her nuns how to make sweets, leather crosses, embroidery and handworks. She learned them all from St Abu Sefein monastery, during her early years of monasticism.

She encouraged the nuns to have one hour of silence where they could recite spontaneous prayers like: "O Lord Jesus Christ, have mercy on me a sinner." Mar Isaac would say:

"Without these spontaneous prayers, we cannot come closer to God."

While they were working, Tamav encouraged them to sing hymns and recite the stories of the saints. By the grace of God, the number of nuns in the monastery slowly increased. Tamav Yoana would encourage every one of them in their monastic path.

Renovations in the Monastery:

The Lord supported Tamav Yoana and allowed the land of the monastery to double. The Lord enlarged and blessed the monastery. This allowed Mother Yoana to accept more nuns and offer more Bridal souls to Jesus.

Tamav started with the ancient church and made two altars, one for St Mary and one for St George. At the beginning, the monastery was just one building with nothing extra. However, when Tamav Yoana became the Abbotess of the monastery, she enlarged the land of the monastery, built churches, cells and gardens. The first time they prayed in the churches was on 1st May 1991, which coincided with St George Feast.

Gradually the monastery constituted of six buildings. It also had a doctor clinic, a pharmacy, a dental clinic and a room for baking the Holy bread. A very high fence wall surrounded the whole monastery.

Mother Yoliana, the eldest nun in the monastery, departed in 1996 at the age of 90. She said a story: Tamav Yoana entered the monastery and became a nun at the time when Mother Mariam was the Abbotess of the monastery. After Mother Mariam departed, Mother Yoliana cried severely due to the loss of her spiritual mother. Mother Yoliana saw Mother Mariam in a dream. Mother

Mariam asked her why she was crying badly, so she said: "I want to come to you, ask God so he can take me quickly."

Mother Mariam said: "What are you saying; it is still early for you. You are still young and you will be alive till you see the 4th head of the monastery and you will see the monastery double during her time."

Truly Mother Yoliana lived during the times of Tamav Mariam, Tamav Kereya Boules, Kereya Eskander and the fourth mother, Tamav Yoana. She saw all the renovations and she said: "I lived and I saw what Mother Mariam told me about."

After Mother Yoana finished with the building in Old Cairo, she bought a land 70 Acres in Khatatba in October 1994. She used this land for plantations. The strange thing was that she was looking for land for a long time. When she saw this land in 1991, she liked it but it was too expensive. She continued looking for land but she still did not like any of the lands she saw. The piece of land she liked was sold but the person who bought it, later returned the land and took his money back. Therefore, Mother Yoana was able to buy this land, as though the Lord was preserving this land for her.

The land was used for plantations and the raising of cattle and chicken. Addition buildings were also built. Pope Shenouda opened it on the 20th of April 2000, three weeks after her departure. Pope Shenouda was saying how hard Tamav Yoana worked as a lot of effort was put into building this place. All the people felt the blessings of Tamav Yoana.

"For they perceived that this work was done by our God." (Nehemiah 6:16)

His Holiness Pope Shenouda ordained 55 nuns into her

monastery, happening four times during her ordination.

Mother Yoana paid special care to the feast of St George which was celebrated three times each year. St George departed on 1st of May, the transfer of his relics occurred on 23rd of July and the consecration of his church on 16th of November. Tamav always wanted people to benefit from these celebrations. Enormous amounts of people would gather at the monastery on the feasts of St George.

Chapter 6

Some of Her Virtues
&
Personal Characteristics

Everyone who knew Tamav Yoana was astonished at the amount of virtues she possessed. She was a lady of high spirituality, strong love, honest service, simplicity, wisdom, kindness, strength, firmness, gentleness and courage.

She was successful in everything because she always lived with God. Tamav Yoana established all these virtues, with humility being her foundation.

Humility

The obvious virtue in the life of Tamav Yoana is the virtue of humility. It was obvious to everyone and it touched anyone who dealt with her.

Mother Yoana lived the life of self-denial, taking her example from St Mary. She always meditated on the life of St Mary and always advised her nuns to do the same. Mother Yoana's life was full of humility.

One day, one of the Bishops came in to the monastery and Tamav Yoana saw him at the entry door. She didn't recognise him but she looked after him with humility and love. The bishop did not know she was the head nun until one of the nuns came and called her Tamav. At that time he noticed how humble she was.

It was very easy for Tamav Yoana to say phrases like, "I am sorry" and "It is my sin." She always said them in a very humble way.

She strongly refused any word of complement from anyone,

especially in her work and her establishments in the monastery. She would always say, "I haven't done anything. It is the house of God and He does all the work." She always gave herself up for others, becoming a role model in all things.

Sometimes she would clean the bathrooms and when a beginner nun would ask her why, she would say that all the other nuns have been working hard and that she is in need of the blessing.

One day when the workers were painting the bathrooms, they left empty cups and dirty paint all over the place. Tamav Yoana took these cups and washed them thoroughly. She asked one of the nuns to take them and put them away in their place. She did everything in humility, love and silence, without ordering any one to do it.

She always worked with her hands. In 1983, the monastery land was completely full of thorns and weeds, but after great effort and continuous work, she transferred it into a beautiful garden.

One day, after the Kiahk praises, all the nuns had slept, yet a nun saw Mother Yoana stay up, cleaning the windows. When the nun questioned her, Mother Yoana said that the windows were dirty and needed a clean.

Mother Yoana always said, "I am poor and weak." She always said this phrase, up until her departure. "As much as one humiliates himself and refuses himself, as much as the Lord glorifies him."

Gentleness and Calmness

Everyone knew of the gentleness and calmness of Tamav Yoana. If she ever talked, it would be out of necessity.

"A word fitly spoken is like apples of gold in settings of silver."

(Proverbs 25: 11)

She was gentle in her words, never talked with firmness or authority. "Learn from Me, for I am gentle and lowly in heart, and you will find rest for your souls." (Mat 11:29)

Mother Yoana taught her nuns that the mouth that praises God will never blurt out an unsuitable word, even if it was targeting an enemy. She was always polite in requesting others to do certain tasks. The nun would easily accept to do anything as a result of Tamav's profound gentleness.

She always respected the elder mothers and put them as her first priority. She taught the younger nuns to do the same. Whenever Tamav had to be firm, she never raised her voice or showed any sign of tension or annoyance. Whenever she had to discuss something with a nun, she would visit her by night and talk gently about the mistake in hand.

With her gentleness, she touched the heart of all visitors. Everyone would say: "Who can see her and not love her?" She even touched the heart of children and many parents decided to name their children after this blessed nun.

One of the nuns was saying that just before she entered the monastery, her mother was harshly preventing her from becoming a nun. She informed Tamav Yoana of the situation. Tamav addressed the mother with a warm heart and smile. Tamav told the mother: "Do you accept me to be a mother for your daughter." After the mother saw the gentleness of Tamav and her beautiful words, she allowed her daughter to enter the monastery in joy.

In another incident, one of the nuns came to the monastery without her family being aware. She sent a letter to her family telling them that she was not coming back. Her father was very emotional and came to the monastery with the rest of the family. The whole family cried a lot. The father tried to take his daughter back but when he saw Tamav, he changed completely. He smiled and said, "I was coming to take my daughter back but after I met you, I wanted to take a holiday from the world and come stay here with you too."

One day, a woman came to the monastery and kept attacking it. As she was checking out the monastery, she fainted. The nuns ran to her and performed first aid. Tamav dealt with her in love and gentleness, until she recovered. She was taken to the church and given blessed water and oil. The lady was affected by the way the nuns treated her.

Even though she was attacking them, the nuns were pouring love at her feet. Immediately, the lady changed her attitude towards the monastery and became a personal friend to Tamav. "When a man's ways please the Lord, He makes even his enemies to be at peace with him."(Proverbs 16: 7)

When the monastery was being renovated, Brasky Aziz the builder, had a quarrel with the engineer, Gamil Foad, regarding the prices he would accept for his work.

Tamav heard the quarrel but remained silent. When Braky asked Tamav, "Are you happy with this quarrel," Tamav answered calmly and said: "You will take blessings from the monastery. This is more valuable than anything money can offer. However, if you still want to increase the price paid, we can increase it." The man accepted the original wage, confident in the blessings he would receive from the monastery.

Her Love

Tamav loved the Lord very much from her heart. This love spread to everyone around her and people noticed it. People used to call her "Tamav Love."

It was not love by word but by action. She was a true mother, a gift from heaven. She was always kind to her daughters in the monastery and cared for each one, meeting their needs and problems. She was their mother, in both flesh and spirit.

She always felt for the needy and sick. She loved and cared for those in tribulation, agony and sadness. Her heart was open to all. Her calm face gave comfort to those in distress. Her love removed any fear. She always reminded people that: "The most important thing in the world is our love to God and our love to each other."

When one of the nuns had hypoglycaemia (low blood sugar), Tamav would stay up all night with her until she would get better. She could give that job to any other nun, but she never did, because of the motherly heart that she carried.

When one of the nuns had an operation, Tamav would go see her in the hospital. If the nun was in pain, Mother Yoana would be greatly affected. She would cry back to the monastery and ask all the nuns to pray for this sick and pained nun. Her heart was very compassionate towards the sick. She would visit them and do anything in her way to help them. "I was sick and you visited Me." (Matt 25: 36)

She always encouraged her daughters to love and serve till the second mile. She would say: "Try to receive blessings from everyone. Serve everyone to attain blessing. Any nice word, hidden work or smile, will offer a blessing, more precious than any treasure the world can give."

Tamav Yoana always cared for the materialistic needs of her spiritual daughters. She would enter into their cells and meet their needs without them asking.

Tamav always practiced this verse: "Let us consider one another in order to stir up love and good works." (Hebrews 10: 24)

Out of her love, she allowed her spiritual daughters to visit some of the other ancient monasteries for retreat. She allowed them to go to places like St Anthony monastery, St Paul monastery and Anba Samuel monastery, where they would obtain the blessings of these places. She always tried to gather her daughters together in a love meeting.

Her Mercy

The heart that is filled with love overflows with mercy, as the Bible says: "Therefore, as the elect of God, holy and beloved, put on tender mercies, kindness, humility, meekness, longsuffering." (Colossians 3:12)

Mother Yoana opened the door of the monastery to all the poor people. She organised monthly payments to help the poor, especially during feasts. She also supplied them with medicines from the monastery pharmacy.

She looked after those who had no one to remember them. She supported many people during their difficult times. She was never greedy to give money. "He who has pity on the poor, lends to the Lord, And He will pay back what he has given." (Proverbs 19:17)

On one occasion, Tamav realised that one of the workers were not feeling normal. She inquired and found that he was experiencing financial issues. Tamav gave him some money, yet the man refused to take it. After Tamav insisted, he took part of the amount and asked for Tamav's prayers. A week later, the man found a good job and his financial situation improved.

One of the nuns said: "When my sister came from Upper Egypt to have an operation, I took permission from Tamav to visit her in the hospital. Tamav accepted and even accompanied me. She also asked the monastery to prepare a meal which would be sent to my sister every day in hospital. Truly, it is true love flowing from a motherly heart." "Blessed is he who considers the poor; The Lord will deliver him in time of trouble." (Psalm 41: 1)

Her Firmness:

Although Mother Yoana was gentle and calm, she was also firm. She discerned between darkness and light. Despite her love and kindness, she was never lenient with any of her sister nuns, regarding monastic rule and tradition. She was firm in guiding, directing and teaching them. She did this to help the nuns grow higher in their spiritual life.

Her firmness and love made everyone fear and respect her. One day, one of the nuns made a mistake in one of the jobs. When Tamav addressed this issue, the nun said: "It is not me; I am not responsible for it."

When Tamav heard her response, she looked to her firmly and told her: "Did we learn to answer that way; did we learn to put the blame on others? We have to blame ourselves."

This was a lesson for everyone.

Tamav was very cautious about the spiritual life of her

daughters. She organised to sit with every nun monthly to make sure that each nun was progressing in her spiritual life.

Her smile and Joy in the Lord

Tamav Yoana always had a smiley face. This gave peace to everyone who saw her. The church fathers used to say: "The humble person always has a smiley face and this smile never leaves him."

The peace of the Lord filled her heart and this was portrayed in her character. Her happiness was a fruit of the Holy Spirit.

"But the fruit of the Spirit is love, joy, peace, longsuffering, kindness, goodness, faithfulness, gentleness, self-control." (Galatians 5:22-23)

She never liked to see anyone sad, but constantly encouraged her daughters to smile. With her smile, she gained the souls of many people. Her joyful countenance was full of hope and comfort.

Her love for prayer

Her life was full of prayer. Her love for prayer left a mark on every soul. She respected prayer and always stood before the Lord in absolute fear and reverence.

When she prayed her spontaneous prayers, her words were full of depth, love and submission. This was a source of peace and comfort to everyone who heard her pray. Her prayers ascended to the Lord with a beautiful aroma of incense.

When Tamav Yoana was a nun in St Abu Sefein monastery, Tamav Irini felt her blessings all the time.

Tamav Irini usually sent for her whenever there was a major problem. Mother Yoana would pray over the problem and light a candle. She would put all problems before the Lord, confident that the Lord would intervene.

"I will instruct you and teach you in the way you should go; I will guide you with My eye." (Psalm 32:8)

Every Tuesday, the Late Rev. Father Angelos, the Syrian would pray a Mass. The Holy Bread would have to be prepared from the previous day. On one occasion, Tamav forgot to arrange for that and remembered only at midnight. She stood up and prayed, asking the Lord to organise this issue. In the morning, she sent two nuns to find a nearby church that was holding a mass. At that time, no churches would hold masses on Tuesday.

However, when the nuns arrived to St George church, which was near the monastery, they found Mr Fekry (the Holy Bread maker) who said, "The offertory is ready for you mothers." The nuns were astonished. They asked him how he knew of their need for Holy Bread. He said that a nun had come to him last night and told him to prepare the offertory as they would be picked up the next day. The two nuns took the offertory and glorified the Lord.

Another incident: In one of the celebration feasts of St George, Tamav wanted to install more lights in the monastery, but the Archaeology organisation refused it and took off the lights. Tamav Yoana was upset from St George so she told him, "Will you leave us like this? Why don't you lighten the monastery yourself?" Tamav left the matter in front of St George, confident that he will never leave his monastery. Indeed, the Lord was glorified.

Instead of the small light that the archaeology had previously refused; heavy lights were installed at their expense.

"And the king granted them to me according to the good hand of my God upon me." (Nehemiah 2:8)

During the last days of her life, when her health was deteriorating and she could not tolerate hearing any more details or problems, it was enough for her to lift her heart and pray. The Lord always answered her prayers. Truly, "The effective, fervent prayer of a righteous man avails much." (James 5:16)

Tamav was very profound in her spirituality. Her spirit constantly accompanied her words and worked in all souls who listened to her. Her words were few, yet powerful as the Bible says:

"The lips of the righteous feed many." (Proverbs 10:21)

"Take counsel, execute judgment; Make your shadow like the night in the middle of the day." (Isaiah 16:3)

Tamav Yoana gathered her daughters daily and would read for them from the scrolls of Anba Pachomious and St John the ladder. Sometimes she gathered them for spiritual meetings, where they would discuss a specific virtue like love or humility. In this meeting, she usually answered their questions with an open mind, open heart and great love.

She also gathered the nuns for Bible study. Tamav Yoana was well known for her strong love of the Holy Bible. Ever since her services in Sunday school, she loved to contemplate and study the Holy Bible. The solitude and silence of monasticism helped her enjoy and live the words of the Bible. She became a living Bible.

During her time at St Abu Sefein monastery, Tamav Irini would give Mother Yoana the responsibility of preparing Bible study meetings once a week. Tamav Yoana continued to do this, even after taking responsibility over St George monastery. She would gather the nuns and give them a deep, meditative, spiritual insight into the Bible.

His Holiness Pope Shenouda, was her confession father, since

1963. Consequently, she was trained by him. He taught her the life of monasticism and trusted her by giving her responsibility over an Italian nun who came to Egypt to study Coptic monasticism in the Coptic Orthodox Church.

The Italian nun arrived in the monastery and stayed from 17/11/1994 to 16/08/1995, under the care and guidance of Tamav Yoana. The Italian nun was greatly affected by the life of Coptic monasticism that she extended her stay, after taking approval from her monastery in Italy.

Even the abbotess of the monastery in Italy came to visit the monastery in Old Cairo and was touched by the love of Tamav Yoana.

"Let another man praise you, and not your own mouth; A stranger, and not your own lips." (Proverbs 17:2)

The Italian nun implemented some of the systems she learned from Coptic monasticism in her monastery in Italy. She continues to communicate with the monastery until now.

Tamav Yoana's motherhood had no limit as she looked after the spirituality of the workers in the monastery as well. She brought a blessed father, to whom they could confess to. She also prepared a special mass for them every month. After the mass, she would invite them for an Aghapy meal and distribute presents among them. If she knew of a worker who smoked, she would talk to him gently about how smoking damages both body and spirit. She would continually pray for him, never giving up until he would quit.

During 1981, there were many families who had lost their fathers in arrest. As a result of her love, she would open the door of the monastery to these families at any time and she would spend feast days with them.

Tamav Yoana served everybody, guiding, teaching and loving them.

One of the daughters in Tamav Yoana's Sunday school class said: "I came to the monastery and I was tired because of my problems with my mother–in-law. When I complained to Tamav Yoana, she talked to me with a few words but it was beneficial for my comfort and my salvation. She told me, "Remember our lesson in Sunday school about how Ruth used to serve Naomi?"

When I went home, I started a new beginning with my mother-in-law as I served her with love until her departure. The house was filled with peace and blessings, by the prayers and guidance of Tamav Yoana."

Another woman who visited the monastery was experiencing lots of arguments with her husband. Tamav always prayed for her and comforted her with words of wisdom. With Tamav's help, the marital relationship was eventually strengthened and filled with peace.

The words of Tamav were few, yet deep and a cause of salvation for many.

On one occasion, there was a girl suffering from many tribulations, causing her to weaken in faith. The girl's mother was very bitter in soul so she went to Tamav Yoana, seeking help. Tamav Yoana was affected by the situation, and calmed the mother with her love and kindness. She promised the mother that she would pray for her daughter. Tamav knew of the power of prayer, so she asked all the nuns to raise special prayers for this young girl, and fast for three days. The Lord was glorified and the young girl strengthened in faith again.

Out of her motherly love, Tamav Yoana shared with others in all their life circumstances and problems.

"Rejoice with those who rejoice, and weep with those who weep." (Romans 12:15)

The life of Submission

Tamav Yoana lived a life of absolute submission as she had strong faith in the Lord, loved Him and consecrated all her life to Him.

Since childhood, she trained to be submissive and grew with this mentality. She submitted her life to God when her father refused to allow her to go to University. She submitted and obeyed when her father refused her consecration in St George monastery and forced her out.

She submitted her life to the Lord, knowing that He would organise everything in His time. The Lord knew the burning desire in her heart and allowed her to join the consecrated house, where she got to learn on the hands of Pope Shenouda, the confession father of the house at the time. She grew in monastic virtues under His guidance. As a result of yielding to the Lord's will, her years at the consecrated house helped her enter into St Abu Sefein monastery, which also prepared her for the leadership role she would take at St George monastery.

When she became the abbotess of St George monastery, her submissive heart prevented her from fearing anything. Whenever the monastery faced an issue, especially a financial issue, Tamav Yoana would respond to the problem lightly, confident that the monastery was the Lord's house and any problem in it, was the

Lord's responsibility.

"Delight yourself in the Lord, and He shall give you the desires of your heart. Commit your way to the Lord, trust also in Him, and He shall bring it to pass." (Psalm 37:4-5)

When Tamav wanted to buy more land for the monastery, the monastery did not have enough money to pay the instalments, yet with her strong faith, she knew that the Lord would create a pathway.

Later on, all the instalments were paid and a high fence around the land, was also afforded. The land became blessed and witnessed to the grace of God and the submission of Tamav Yoana.

"Truly this is the blessing of the Lord." (Proverbs 10:22)

Simplicity And Purity Of Heart

Since her childhood, Tamav Yoana always struggled to attain purity of heart. She always recalled this verse: "Blessed are the pure in heart, for they shall see God." (Matthew 5:8)

She always taught her nuns, that the pure heart does not get angry or affected by any external circumstance. When the heart is humble and pure, everything can be relieved.

Anyone who lived with Tamav, would see her purity of heart. Her purity made her an ambassador of heaven, not merely a human on earth. Her thoughts were always focused on heaven and the love of God. She had a special love for little children, dealing with them in love and innocence. The feeling became mutual as the children knew her more. "Let the little children come to Me, and do not forbid them; for of such is the kingdom of heaven." (Matthew 19:14)

Bearing Pain With Patience And Thanksgiving

Tamav Yoana lived her life and carried her cross in Joy. When the cross became heavier, she increased in her patience and endurance. During her childhood, she bore pains from her mother who prevented her from leaving the house, unlike any other child her age.

In her youth, she bore pains from her father who was very strict and prevented her from continuing with a university education. These crosses were tough but the Lord gave Tamav much grace and strength. The Lord reigned in her heart and He became her one goal in life. She never focused on any worldly or earthly desire.

Tamav also carried the cross of rejection, when her parents rejected her desire for monasticism. She lived as the Bible says:

"You therefore must endure hardship as a good soldier of Jesus Christ." (2 Timothy 2:3) She carried all her crosses with love and honesty as the Bible says: "Whoever desires to come after Me, let him deny himself, take up his cross and follow Me."

(Mark 8:34)

She bore the cross of responsibility with thankfulness and silence. She was responsible for the salvation of many nuns, doing her best to protect them from satanic attacks.

In her sufferings, she never troubled anyone or bothered them with her pain.

On one occasion, she was working in the garden when a long thorn pricked her foot. She bore the pain until she finished with her gardening. However, she started to limp. When the Doctor assessed her, he removed the thorn and was surprised at how Tamav could bear all that pain, without stopping work and seeking help.

Another incident happened where she sprained her leg and fractured a bone in her foot. Despite her pain, she went to the monasteries church to do glorification praises for St George. She stood throughout the entire prayer, without anyone noticing that she was in pain.

Tamav always bore the cross of pain in thanksgiving and praise.

"For in that He Himself has suffered, being tempted, He is able to aid those who are tempted." (Hebrews 2:18)

Tamav Yoana lived the life of virtues. She was a fruitful garden that heaven loved. The saints always supported and surrounded her.

Dr Sabri Soliman, a Dentist who visited the monastery, recorded this incident himself: "On the night of St George feast in 1989, I came to the monastery with my very close friend. During the vesper prayers, my friend saw St George on his horse. He was riding around several houses that were located near the monastery. He kept insisting that the monastery was to buy these houses. He then got off his horse, walked to the garden and stopped. Indeed, several years later, the monastery had bought and renovated these houses and the place where St George had gotten off his horse, had become a church."

Dr Sabri continued by saying: "My friend did not know anything about Mother Yoana. During the procession of St George, he saw many angels surrounding Mother Yoana in joy and glory. She was standing in the middle of them and her face was full of light."

Dr Sabri said: "I was standing beside my friend and I did not know why he looked so surprised and shocked. When he calmed down, he pointed to Tamav Yoana and told me that this nun must have attained a high level of holiness."

Truly, Tamav Yoana was a humble person who lived a life of self-denial. She always worked in secret, doing everything out of pure love for God.

Her sickness

The Lord looked to his chosen bride and saw that she was increasing in virtue. He wanted to purify her more so He crowned her with the cross of sickness in her last few years on earth. She accepted the cross with thanksgiving and patience. "The spirit of a man will sustain him in sickness." (Proverbs 18:14)

She increased in humility more and more and her sweetness became more sweet and pure. "Blessed are those who are drunk by Your love O Lord. This drunkenness makes them forget their old life." (St John)

She lived her last days as an angel on earth. Nothing ever interrupted or affected her. She lived a life of continuous prayer, in conjunction with the Saints.

She always kept the Words of the Lord on her tongue. She continuously prayed and said: "My Lord Jesus Christ, have mercy on me a sinner" and "My Lord Jesus Christ give me a heart of repentance."

She always called on St Mary, Archangel Michael, St George, St Abanoub and St Abraam. She never wanted anything to disrupt her secret relationship with God. She always taught her daughters: "From your work to your cell to your prayers." All her thoughts and all her words were pure. She never tolerated anything outside the Holy teachings of the Bible.

"Blessed is the man who trusts in the lord and whose hope is the Lord, For he shall be like a tree planted by the waters, Which spreads out its roots by the river, And will not fear when heat comes; But its leaf will be green, And will not be anxious in the year of drought, Nor will cease from yielding fruit." (Jeremiah 17:7)

During her moments of severe pain, she would always sing hymns of praise to the Lord. The name of Jesus never left her tongue, but was a source of strength during her weakest times. The night before her departure was spent entirely in hospital. She kept saying: "Lord Jesus have mercy on me a sinner, Lord Jesus help me repent. Lord Jesus, I love you very much. Lord Jesus, I love you more than any other person. Virgin Mary, help me."

When a non-Christian nurse asked her "Do you love me mother?" She answered: "Yes I love you very much. I love all people very much." Even during her times of pain, her love reigned and her peace was transferred to all those who saw her.

Whenever she saw one of her daughters, she would tell her: "Love one another." She would also say: "You are all lovely; all of you are Saints," giving each nun a lesson of how she should view and esteem her sister.

Her sickness did not let her forget her motherhood to all the nuns. She was always sensitive to the affairs of each nun. She could feel what each nun was going through; the spirit of God never left her.

The brother of one of the nuns was getting married. This nun wished in her heart that Tamav would pray for the wedding and bless it. When Tamav came down from her cell, she held the hands of this nun and told her: "Just Pray Our Father." The nun was amazed that Tamav had felt for her.

On another occasion, one of the nuns was serving but she

doubted if she would get a reward in heaven or not. Tamav came to her and told her: "Your reward will be great in heaven." The nun was filled with comfort.

Another time, a disagreement occurred between two nuns. One of the nuns headed to Tamav, asking her a random question. Tamav told her: "Go reconcile with your sister first as nothing is better than love." The nun was surprised at how Tamav may have known about the disagreement. She apologised to Tamav and reconciled with her sister, performing a prostration before her. Truly, the Holy Spirit was always working in the heart of Tamav.

Even if the flesh is sick and old, the spirit will never weaken as long as the Holy Spirit dwells inside.

Her Departure

Tamav Yoana was always thankful in her sickness. She never stopped praising and lifting her eyes up to heaven. She experienced much colic pain. She was transferred to hospital on Tuesday 28th March 2000, where the doctors decided to have an immediate operation.

After a week, the Lord wanted to crown her and give her rest from all her sufferings as He found that His bride had fought the good fight, finished the race and kept the faith. On Tuesday 4th April 2000, at 2pm, she had a heart attack where her pure soul was taken up to heaven. She enjoyed the Bridal Wedding, amidst the angels and saints whom she loved.

Her holy body was transferred to the church of the monastery at 4pm. All the nuns were upset by the loss of their mother. They took her blessings and started to praise and pray Tasbeha. During that time the news spread regarding her departure so many people came to take her blessings. The nuns prayed the whole Tasbeha in front of the Holy body 4 times. They also spent the night reading the book of Revelations, Psalms, Gospel of St John and the Epistle of St Paul to the Corinthians. At 6am, early morning, Anba Sherobim, Bishop of Kena, prayed the Holy Mass with other priests. At 10am, His Holiness Pope Shenouda came to pray on her Holy Body. He was accompanied by 12 other bishops:

His eminence metropolitan Domadious, Bishop of El Giza

His grace Bishop Reweis, the General Bishop

His grace Bishop Mattaous, Abbott of St Mary Elsourian monastery.

His grace Bishop Botros, the General Bishop.

His grace Bishop Basanti, Bishop of Helwan and El Maasara.

His grace Bishop Mettias, Bishop of Mahala el Kobra

His grace Bishop Daniel, Bishop of Maadi churches

His grace Bishop Yohanna, Bishop of Old Cairo Churches.

His grace Bishop Yoannas, the secretary of His Holiness.

His grace Bishop Rafaeel, Bishop of middle city centre churches.

His grace Ghobrial, the General Bishop.

Many fathers the priests also attended the funeral, as well as the Reverent Tamav Irini, the Abbotess of St Abu Sefein monastery, Reverent Tamav Mariam, the Abbotess of St Mary monastery and many nuns. It was a very affectionate farewell.

At the end of the prayer, the nuns carried the coffin with tears and went around the church 3 times, singing hymns and celebrating with the new intercessor that heaven had just received.

Now our dear Mother can repeat with St Paul the Apostle:

"You know...in what manner I always lived among you, serving the Lord with all humility, with many tears ...how I kept back nothing that was helpful, but proclaimed it to you, and taught you publicly." (Acts 20: 18-21)

Blessed are you our Mother for you taught us much and sacrificed much for our sake. We are grateful for the blessing that you delivered and we will continue to collect from the fruits of your work and toil. You may have departed us by flesh, but your spirit has not departed our hearts. Your love and role model will be set before us. You are still among your daughters in faith, spirit and prayer.

The readings on her day of Departure

The reading of Tuesday from the fifth week of the Lent.

(Proverbs 3: 19-34, 4:1-9)

"Give attention to know understanding; For I give you good doctrine: Do not forsake my law. When I was my father's son, Tender and the only one in the sight of my mother, He also taught me, and said to me: Let your heart retain my words; Keep my commands, and live. Get wisdom! Get understanding! Do not forget, nor turn away from the words of my mouth. Do not forsake her, and she will preserve you; Love her, and she will keep you. Wisdom is the principal thing; Therefore get wisdom. And in all your getting, get understanding. Exalt her, and she will promote you; She will bring you honour, when you embrace her. She will place on your head an ornament of grace; A crown of glory she will deliver to you."

Tamav Yoana learned and lived by the commandments since her childhood, so her life was full of wisdom.

(Isaiah 40: 1-8)

"Comfort, yes, comfort My people! Says your God. Speak comfort to Jerusalem, and cry out to her, That her warfare is ended, That her iniquity is pardoned; For she has received from the Lord's hand Double for all her sins."

Tamav Yoana had completed her struggle on earth. The day of her departure was the day of her comfort, her escape from all the pains of the world.

(Catholicon: 1 John 3:2-11)

"Beloved, now we are children of God; and it has not yet been revealed what we shall be, but we know that when He is revealed, we shall be like Him, for we shall see Him as He is. And everyone who has this hope in Him purifies himself, just as He is pure."

Blessed Tamav Yoana, you finally lived for that hope, attaining what you have always strived for. The Lord washed you and purged you, moulded you into a perfect bride for a perfect Groom.

(John 8:12-20)

"Then Jesus spoke to them again, saying, I am the light of the world. He who follows Me shall not walk in darkness, but have the light of life."

Tamav followed the Lord Christ as she lived in light of His Commandments and departed to the continuous light.

The Apparition At The Time Of Her Departure:

One of the ladies (known to the monastery) saw Tamav Yoana appearing in an illuminated body on early Tuesday morning on the 4th of April. She was disturbed and felt anxious. The next day, she discovered the news of Tamav's departure. Tamav Yoana had appeared to this lady to give her a joyous farewell.

Zakia Moawad, was a daughter to Tamav Yoana in Sunday school. She said:

"When I knew of the departure of Tamav Yoana, I was in great shock. I went to her coffin at 6pm and I started to cry. I leaned against the coffin and told her: "Tamav, do you feel that I am here? I am your daughter Zakia and I need you." Immediately I smelt an aroma, two people standing beside me, smelt the aroma too. I told Tamav: "Do not forget me."

Her Quiet Time

In commemoration of her second year of monasticism (6/3/1972), Tamav Yoana wrote beautiful contemplations in her diary.

Blessed is your holy name, Blessed is Your work.

Great is Your love, Great is Your humility.

You are the Glorified God of heaven, yet you chose to come down to earth to purify me and purge me and clean me.

I am not worthy Lord of this love. My heart dissolves when it hears of your tender kindness. Out of Your Love, you make me lack nothing. Never did I ask for something that you did not give me. Dear Lord, you gave me so many chances. There is nothing I desire but you.

Have mercy on me a sinner dear Lord. I have no excuse for my sins, but I know your mercies are bountiful. Truly Lord, you loved me and followed me wherever I went. You called me by day and by night. O Lord, I do not deserve this love. I do not know how to love you in return. Your love is beyond measure.

Dear Lord, my ego prevents me from binding to you and I am sick of it. It becomes my idol and I worship it instead of you. It blinds me and stops me from seeing you. It darkens my mind and stops me from knowing you. It occupies my mind and stops me from thinking of you. If I humiliate my ego, I lose my peace. If I praise it, I rejoice and pride intoxicates me.

Because I love myself, I don't love toil and hard work. Because I love myself, I don't want anyone to be better than me.

Because I love myself, I believe in my thoughts and scorn those who do not obey me.

Dear Lord, now I realise that I do not follow You because I love myself.

Dear Lord, your commandments tell me to deny myself, take up my cross and follow You. How can I obey your commandment O Lord? How can I deny myself?

My Lord, I cannot do anything of my own strength, but I ask for Your strength and for Your help. Crush my ego so that Your love can reign inside me. Open my eyes so I can see You dear Lord. Open my eyes so I can see Your glory. What is impossible for me dear Lord, is possible to you.

How many times did I regret my actions. How many times did I cause problems with my decisions. Confess O my soul for you are a sinner and you do not know how to do good. Lord, You know my weakness. Come and help me because wisdom comes from You. Open my eyes, open my heart and open my thoughts with Your knowledge and light. Help me walk the path You have set before me and help me see my ignorance.

When I depend on myself, I fall many times, but now I trust in You and I submit myself into Your hands. I submit to the guidance of my loving Abbotess and I submit to the guidance of my confession father.

Show me Yourself Lord, so I may know You more and love You more and serve You more.

Dear Lord, let me love You like You loved me. Bind me to You and let me know You more and more. Inflame my emotions with Your love and open my eyes so I can see You, taste You and enjoy You. Allow me to love You with all my heart, my mind, my strength and my power. I want You to be my All in All.

Raise my thoughts so I may think of you always. Let my soul rejoice with You and let my heart dissolve in Your love. Make me forget the world and the things in the world and the people of the world, so I may love and enjoy You.

Grant me to love You and listen to Your words as my soul thirsts for You. Offer me one drop of Your love and let this drop flow like a river inside me, quenching me and creating me anew.

In the memory of the fourth year of her monasticism 6/3/1975.

Dear Lord, although my day was very busy today, You did not leave me, but calmed my soul. I felt very happy because I could feel you with me. I always want to open up my heart to you and talk to you about everything. Please strengthen me in the path you have called me to.

My Lord Jesus, you always look after me because I am so

precious to you. You redeemed my life with Your blood, you loved me, you called me, you took me as your own. O Lord, who am I to deserve all this? I want to offer myself to You. Truly, I am full of faults and defects, but I know You will clean me and purify me and sanctify me, make me fit to be Your bride.

My Lord Jesus, I have given up thinking about myself because I know that my life is entrusted within Your hands. I know that Your hands are capable of changing me and making me holy. I cannot be holy on my own for "unless the Lord builds the house, they labour in vain who build it; unless the Lord guards the city, the watchman stays awake in vain."

My precious Jesus, I am in Your hand. You loved me since the beginning and You knew me before the creation of Man. You carved me on the palm of Your hands and You died on the cross to show me Your love. Dear Lord, You purified me by Your precious Blood and You purged me by the water of Baptism. You made me holy and You can never leave me to stray from You.

O Lord, You feed me with Your holy body and Your holy blood and You anoint me with your Holy Mayroun. You dress me in righteous clothes and You make me beautiful for You. If I run away, You are responsible for returning me. If I become dirty, You clean me with hyssop. If I am thirsty, You refresh me in a fountain of life. If I am hungry, I will find food in You as You are the one who fills me and keeps me alive. If I am sick, I find treatment in You. You are the Doctor of my soul as You revive me every time I start to die.

Dear Lord, I want to be busy with You. I want to be occupied by You alone. How do I draw my thoughts from the vanishing world and focus them on You? How do I extinguish my passionate desires and feelings so I can free myself and bind with You?

I cannot overcome the enemy Lord, unless You show me Yourself. Allow me to see You and connect with You. Every time I taste Your beauty, I start to love you more and more.

Open my eyes to see You and to enjoy You because You are the most stunning of all human beings, beautiful in all Your characters, never ending. You are the Almighty; merciful, kind, meek and great. You are the Creator, the Saviour, the Loving. I cannot describe You dear Lord. Show me Yourself, show me Your characters so I can engross myself in You.

Amazing Lord are Your works and wisdom. I cannot see You but blessed are the pure in heart for they shall see You.

O Lord, You cleanse me, purify me and enlighten my eyes. When I think of You, my thoughts become Holy and my heart cannot stop but ring Your praise. I thank you Lord for this.

Dear Lord, my mother superior always told me: "Meditate on the love of the Lord, on His humility and His characters. Think of Him always, and submit yourself in His hands."

My confession father always told me: "Keep yourself occupied with the Lord and talk to Him continuously, while you sit, while you walk and while you work. All of these will inflame your heart and put you in the front of your spiritual life."

O Lord, I never realised how deep these words were until I stopped thinking about myself and occupied my thoughts with You. Dear Lord, I can gain nothing by myself. Please help me enter into the depths and occupy my heart and my mind and my thoughts with You alone, You alone dear Lord.

Whenever I think of You, I never have time to think about

myself. I see everything to be vain and worthless. Nothing is more precious than spending time with You O Lord. The devil makes me sin so he can steal away my heart from You. He wants me to stop thinking about You. He wants to preoccupy my thoughts with the world.

O Virgin St Mary, Mother of True Light, you are the one that my soul desires. You have kept all the words of God in your heart. You fasted from the world because your One desire was heaven and love towards Your God.

O Mother of Light, teach me how to forget everything and bind with the One. Teach me how to forget myself and join with Your Loving Son, my Lord, God and Saviour Jesus Christ.

Intercede on my behalf, O Mother of Light, so that the Lord can make all my thoughts holy for Him. Intercede on my behalf so that the Lord can inflame my emotions towards Him and reveal Himself to me. To Him be all the Glory, Power, Dominion and Worship now and forever more Amen.

SECTION 2

Sayings From a Contemporary Nun

Chapter 1

Her Sayings

On Monasticism, she said:

Monasticism is the Holy of Holies. It is the life of Paradise because the monk has left the whole world and its pleasures for the sake of God. The monk spends all his time with Jesus, as though in paradise. That is why our church calls the monks, earthly angels or heavenly humans.

The word monk or nun means "Fear of God" because a monk/nun walks in God's fear, according to God's commands, feeling afraid to do anything that deprives them from God.

Monasticism is not about wearing special clothes or belonging to a monastery. Monasticism signifies a monk that has left the world and looked to rejoice in heaven. While he is in the monastery, he will remember the heavenly Jerusalem. When he changes his name, he will remember the saint's name that he took.

It is not enough for a monk to say psalms but rather to praise the Lord continuously. He has to delve deeper into his spiritual life and soar higher into virtue. Even if he is with people, the praise of God should not be stopped.

Monasticism is "the INNER glory of the King's daughter." Her inner soul is full of hidden treasures and secrets to her Beloved. Her life is love and knowledge.

On the importance of prayers, she said:

Go deep in your prayers and every time you see yourself small, move closer to God and He will protect you.

In his prayers, the monk does not feel the pain of the flesh. He does not care about his surroundings and is not affected by it. However the weak person is affected by his surroundings, being tempted by daydreams and pains.

Every time the devil sees a monk kneeling for prayer, he tempts him with sickness, dizziness and weakness in his legs, but this is the struggle. The monk has to realise the devil's tricks and pray all the time, no matter what. If he is tired, he has to pray, if he is fatigued, he has to pray and if he struggles to open his eyes, he still has to pray. Truly, when the Lord sees him struggling, He will relieve him from his struggle, comfort him and confine him into the depth of prayer. However, if the monk gets tired and surrenders to fatigue, the devil will understand that this monk is the type who has pity on himself.

In order to reach the depth of prayer, one must humble himself before God, think himself as nothing and love all people unconditionally.

If my brother makes a mistake, I must not condemn him as God is the only Judge. Instead, I must remember my many weaknesses. The one who judges others can never find comfort in his prayers. He must humble himself, turn a blind eye to other people's sins and live quietly, away from the business of others.

On giving an account one's self, she said:

Sometimes due to the routine in our life, we go astray. In an occasion like this, the person has to examine himself. One must give an account of their and check his principles, just like the prodigal son. The prodigal son thought it was right to leave his home but when he sat alone and thought to himself, he realised he was wrong and returned to his father in repentance. Life with God is pleasant but it requires seriousness and struggle.

One may have certain habits or behaviours that stand in the way of their salvation. Consequently, one must struggle to overcome them. As he forces himself to stop his bad habits, he will start to feel God's comforting presence.

In my struggle, I depend on God. I may face many obstacles, but I am not alone because God strengthens me. I prevent myself from anything that takes me away from God. This can be useless words, irrelevant work or any subject that diverts me from thinking of God.

On obtaining peace and concentrating our heart and minds on heaven, she said:

From time to time, we need to sit alone and think of heaven; how the heavenly souls are living in joy and permanent praise as they see the Lord Jesus Christ, to Him be the glory. The monastery (church) is our heaven on earth, the source of all happiness. If you feel that God is far from you, it could be a result of slackness, busyness, a lack of self-examination or a life of quick prayer, without depth or meaning.

Sometimes the Lord takes away our comfort and peace, for a short period of time, to remind us of the grace and blessings that He always gives us.

Do not let anything occupy you from your goal, which is the love of God. Sometimes secondary things attract our attention more than it should, and so we start wasting our time. We should avoid this, stay close to our God and keep our peace.

Peace leads to joy, uplifts the heart towards God and teaches patience. Even if something provokes from outside, the person with peace will never be affected.

On facing spiritual wars, she said:

During times of tribulation and warfare, a monk must keep his inner peace, no matter what. He should not ask God to take away the tribulation, but he should pray and say: "Without you Lord I cannot do anything, You are the one who teaches me how to fight."

The Lord never leaves the person who knows his weaknesses. Therefore, during time of spiritual warfare, understand your weakness, pray hard and endure with patience. With this, the Lord gives you strength to battle your war. The devil will always want to distract you from your salvation. Know his tricks and never give him the chance. Bear, pass and forgive the sins of others, in order to gain purity of heart. Joy will then appear on your face and shine onto others.

Despite Satanic warfare, life with God is Joy and comfort. Always remember that the enemy is nothing but dust and he has no power over us.

Every time war comes upon you, hold tight onto God and say, "O Lord, I am weak and poor." You will hear the Lord say, "Here I am with you."

The devil aims to put the monk into despair. He tells him, "You are a sinner and you do not deserve to be a monk," but the monk should stand strong in faith, having hope in God's bountiful mercy. God's mercy is huge, more than the sand and water of the sea. With this hope, we can boldly face the wars of our spiritual enemy.

In tribulation, never feel that God is not looking after you. He allows these tribulations according to your ability and after the war, He fills you with comfort and crowns you with glory. Behind every suffering is a beauty. By bearing pain, you share in the pains of your Saviour. To the real Christian, pain has a joyful taste.

On simplicity, she said:

Simplicity is the core of strength. The simple person is full of wisdom and deep love for God. He takes matters easily, his words are comforting and he shifts all his problems onto God. He sees everyone with a simple eye. He bears with others and resorts to prayer whenever faced by a problem.

On living life with Christ, she said:

The Lord Jesus is everything to me. The world never satisfies, yet life with God is full of beauty and splendour. God gives generously to those who choose to live with Him. Out of His great love, He holds every sick and weary person in His right hand. The door of repentance is open. The door into Christ's heart is also open. Listen to His voice, enter into His presence and enjoy the beauty of life with Him. God lives inside each and every one of us, but we never realise it. He offers us His love with bountiful mercy.

Lord draw us near to You because we cannot draw nearby ourselves. If You leave us, we will lose our way in this world.

Chapter 2

Bible Contemplations

Early Spiritual and Monastic Maturity

This sermon was given by Fr Mettaous to a community of monks, four months after his ordination as a monk in the year 1950.

Dear your grace Bishop Theophilus and my dear fathers the priests and monks of the blessed El Sourian Monastery.

I congratulate you on the feast of the Nativity of our Lord Jesus Christ, hoping that He may return these days in growth by His grace, blessings and heavenly gifts, and may He extend the life of our beloved bishop Theophilus. May He grant him growth in the true monastic life, and may He continue the days of spirituality in his days, through his prayers on our behalf, and his deep love towards everyone, and his great humility that inspires us to be like him. May the Lord extend his bishopric reign for many years to come, spending his days in peace and without harm. Through the pleadings of our Lady the Virgin St Mary and St John Kame.

Your Grace, and my respected fellow fathers and brethren, I seek your absolution and forgiveness before I start my talk, as I see myself unworthy to stand in front of you, or to speak to you, for I am a sinner and a weak man.

However, what encouraged me to give this talk is the fact that I am amid my family. Our father Bishop Theophilus blesses us with his presence. For, as a young child, I was accepted in this family, despite my weakness and unworthy state, to speak to you, dear reverends and monks, in the spirit of love, after taking absolution and blessings from my father:

"Glory be to God in the highest, peace on earth, and goodwill towards men."

The angels orchestrated this beautiful song to the shepherds who were vigilant over their flock. Upon entering the manger, they saw the Child wrapped in swaddling cloths, placed in the manger of livestock.

How wonderful that the Creator of Heaven and Earth, to whom every knee in heaven and on earth worship, would humble Himself to come to earth, to the land of misery, to save the creation broken through the sin of the first Adam.

Great news came to us with His miraculous birth. Sing, O my soul, with the angels with this new praise, and learn, O my spirit, the humility of the Creator of the universe and how He was born in a disdained manger.

Truly, how great are these two virtues, which the Lord taught us, among many other virtues, which are Love and Humility:

Firstly, Love: God is love, and out of His love for us, he came down from His highest heaven to wipe away the sin of Adam, and to make us heirs in His inheritence in the glory of His Father. The Bible mentions that He was a Man of great sorrows and experienced in pain. He shared with us everything, except for sin alone. He lived on earth as a man, and in the end He was crucified, was tortured, was placed in a tomb, and arose. Through His resurrection, He broke the gates of Hell and opened the gates of Hades.

Observe, what we should do in return to such great love? Indeed we ought to seek to attain this great love with all our efforts. As monks, through the grace of God, we despised the world and all its lustful desires; we forsook our parents, relatives and friends, and thought about how to attain such love, and what to sacrifice to attain it.

We sought to come to this holy place, where our saintly forefathers lived, and where they attained the highest spiritual level that one can attain, so that their mind and thoughts were in the heavenlies. For a person cannot look at the world with one eye, and with the other eye observe the heavens.

We have living examples of strong personalities, who left behind footsteps for us to follow, that witness to their greatness in the path which they walked in, that is, monasticism.

Monasticism: its sweetness is in its bitterness, and its beauty is apparent. It is delicious to eat; its glories are in heaven. Even though it has many tribulations in its path, and its struggle is difficult, yet when we lift our eyes to the heavenlies, all this pain on earth is worth it.

Therefore, my brethren, let us seek to attain the true love of our beloved Jesus, so that our yearning and enthusiasm may increase, and may the strength of the Lord support us and guide us by His grace.

"My grace is sufficient for you, for My strength is made perfect in weakness."

Secondly, Humility: I am in awe! How can the creation contemplate that the Lord of glory – who spreads out His hands and feeds every living creature – would be born in a disdained and rejected manger. He even said: "Foxes have holes and birds of the air have nests, but the Son of Man has nowhere to lay His head." This was said to teach us a great lesson.

Occasionally I would look at my weak self, when an evil thought bothers me, and I say to myself: "what are you thinking about, poor man? Look at the dust, for it is your mother, and from it you were created, and to it you will return. But look at the prince of the dark hosts, and what rank he was in before he became proud and fell forever."

The Bible mentions the forefathers in their prophetic words, inspired by the Holy Spirit, that without humility, we cannot increase in our spirituality one single step, and therefore we would never reach our goal of the heavenlies.

"Looking unto Jesus, the author and finisher of our faith"

"Whosoever looked upon Him were enlightened, and their faces shall not be ashamed"

We raise our hearts to the Child in the manger, through the prayers of our father Bishop Theophilus – who is a role model for humility – asking God to make us true monks, not just by names, struggling in every virtue with all holiness, godliness, love and humility. May we be worthy to enjoy the heavenly glories with all the saints who struggled and conquered.

Through the pleadings of our Lady the Virgin St Mary, and St John Kame, and all the saints who have pleased you since the beginning with their good deeds. Amen

Happy New Year

From the mouth of the most despised and youngest monk.

7 January 1950

The Last shall be First

"For the kingdom of heaven is like a landowner who went out early in the morning to hire laborers for his vineyard. Now when he had agreed with the laborers for a denarius a day, he sent them into his vineyard. And he went out about the third hour and … Again he went out about the sixth and the ninth hour… And about the eleventh hour he went out and found others standing idle… and he gave them their wages, beginning with the last to the first…But when the first came, they supposed that they would receive more;

and they likewise received each a denarius. And when they had received it, they complained against the landowner... So the last will be first, and the first last. For many are called, but few chosen." (Matt 20: 1-16)

The Lord told us a parable about a man who had a vineyard, who hired labourers for his vineyard. One team started at the first hour, another at the third hour, another at the sixth hour, and another at the ninth hour. Finally, he found idle people at the eleventh hour, so he sent them to work in his vineyard. He had a agreement to pay them one denarii each at the end of the day. We note that the people who got paid first were the last people to come to work, at the eleventh hour, and were made equal with those who started working from the morning.

It might be that the Lord of glory wants to teach us that cursed is the man who does the work of the Lord in vain. The people who came at the eleventh hour, are the people who come into the faith late, and their faith and good deeds bring forth fruit, and become a salt to the earth and a light to the world in a short period of time, and so deserve to receive the good reward like the people who were born in the faith from a young age, and who struggled all their lives to attain the Kingdom. We also hear in the history of monasticism of youth who struggled and excelled beyond elders in virtue. Did not the right hand thief deserve the Kingdom of Heaven, while the disciple perished, despite excelling beyond other believers in the Lord Christ?

The Lord also teaches us about jealousy and envy, which develops in our hearts when we see others excelling in their deeds, and for this reason it was mentioned in the parable that the workers complained against the landowner. The Lord carries the sins of mankind, but He cannot stand jealousy and envy from a man. Disgruntlement indicates their unacceptance of what the Lord has in place for them, which means they are going against the will of the Almighty Lord. It is as if he wants to be in charge of his own life. "Is it not lawful for Me to do what I wish with My own things? Or is your eye evil because I am Good?"

So the "last will be first, and the first last". The Lord also said: "By your patience possess your souls." The life of solitude on this earth is a life of continual struggle with continuous enthusiasm, for monks have been called to this life from the Landowner, to praise and bless and glorify Him continuously, so that they may not deviate from the temptations of the enemy, that they may not lose the path to Heaven.

10 September 1956

"I am the door. If anyone enters by Me, he will be saved, and will go in and out and find pasture." (John 10: 9)

Jesus is the door. Whoever finds Him will be saved, and whoever enters by Him, will go into the deep, and will not reach the bottom of the Lord's consolance and unspeakable mercy.

Is this pasture not the pasture of our fathers the saints, who ate from it, and lived in it, and gave us of its fruits as teachings to fill us? The souls of His beloved find pasture in Him, and they contemplated on the One whom they love, until they understood the secrets of the Kingdom of God, and so they were drunk with His love. They forgot the body, and its pride; not only their thoughts, but their souls transcended up to heaven. They knocked on the door, and the Bridegroom quickly got up to open the door to welcome His bride out of His great love towards her. He could not wait, He was waiting for a groan. There they were filled with the Living Spring that does not run dry. The Lover asked her, 'what do you seek?' (till now you have not asked anything in my Name) Then she took from Him and after that, when she was saved and delivered, she overflowed on others with this treasure of goodness.

9 January 1957

"And when He had looked around at them with anger, being grieved by the hardness of their hearts, He said to the man, "Stretch out your hand." And he stretched it out, and his hand was restored as whole as the other." (Mark 3: 5)

Is this not evidence for obedience? Just the fact that the sick man obeyed the order of the Lord, by stretching out his hand, his hand was healed.

Therefore, obeying the commandments has the power to heal the illnesses of the soul.

9 February 1957

"But He said to them, "It is I; do not be afraid." Then they willingly received Him into the boat, and immediately the boat was at the land where they were going." (John 6: 20-21)

When a person is far away from Jesus, he will be scared and in despair. The empty heart, which God has not reigned over yet, is like a boat in the midst of the sea. But when we open the door for the One standing outside knocking, He will come in and immediately we have reached the harbour of peace and comfort.

13 April 1957

A Fiery Love

Blessed be our God, who redeemed us with His honoured Blood on the cross, thus we were allowed to enter the Holy of Holies in Heaven. That is, through our faith in Him, we were reconciled with His Father, and thus became partakers in the glory. Being sinners , we sought to be set free from the bonds of sin, but we could not. But suddenly He shone inside our hearts with His light, and the darkness was scattered, and His strength set us free from the bonds and so not out of righteous deeds did we attain this freedom, but through His mercy He freely saved us.

The ways of salvation are many, and the ways of asceticism are diverse. Whoever sees a ray of light in his heart, he immediately struggles and forces himself to increase in his level of spirituality and holiness.

The monks have seen and heard many stories of the struggles of great saints, such as St Anthony, St Paul the Hermit, St Bakhomious, St Macarius, and St Shenouda who used to crucify his body on a cross like his master throughout Passion Week. St Paul of Tammouh and St Bishoy, as well as others who worshipped God with their hearts, were enlightened, and thus were able to shine as an example to the generations to come, and to us at this present day.

Many times we would cool off, and try to imitate them, wanting to be like them, but far be it! We forget, or neglect, that these great saints, who fended off the devils and their unseen traps, had a greater goal; their goal in life was 'Love'. How deep is love, even though it is little in letters, but is life in its fullness. All the writers of this world, and even the spiritually enlightened, could never fathom the depth of love with their own understanding, or with their pens. For love is God, and who is able to contain God, or speak about

God? For God is love.

Those people had a burning fire in their hearts, kindled with their love towards Jesus Christ, and so they kindled their works, so that this verse applies to them: "to him who has, more shall be given".

For this reason, prophets came and prophesied. For this reason the commandments were set, and for this reason we were saved as Christians. For this reason our apostles preached and lived the word of God.

The most convincing answer, for anyone who seeks the life of complete surrender and positive struggle is given in the Lord's answer to the lawyer who asked Him which commandment is the greatest? It is: "You shall love the LORD your God with all your heart, with all your soul, and with all your mind.' This is the first and great commandment. And the second is like it: "You shall love your neighbor as yourself.' On these two commandments hang all the Law and the Prophets." (Matt 22: 37-40)

22 May 1957

Is it greed, or the ambition of the soul?

A person is never satisfied in material things for as soon as he achieves something, he starts looking for another target. Sometimes he even tries to leap hurdles in order to reach his aim, when in reality he destroys himself and loses everything. There are two factors related to this: fear and doubt. Fear compels a person, while doubt makes him confused between truth and certainty, and so he stands still and is confused, but remember the words of the Lord "I wish he were hot or cold, but he is lukewarm" (Rev 3: 15).

So, who can reach the harbour peacefully, without deviation? It is the person who doesn't care about the fears and doubts surrounding him. As long as he is sure and comfortable that he is headed steadily for his target, nothing can hold or frighten him. He is always peaceful during the time of war, his heart is enlightened and he is full of inner comfort because he is heading towards his target, God.

This monk is similar to the tortoise that reached the top of the hill before the rabbit. One of the saints said: "I like consistent light work more than vigorous work that would exhaust me quickly and lead me to soon stop." St John Saba once said: "consistent work, even if it is little, is considered as a great treasure which accumulates."

How great are the Lord's mercies! He never abandons those who seek Him and are submissive to His will, "They looked to Him and were radiant, and their faces were not ashamed" (Ps 34:5).

In the midst of darkness He lights our inner soul, dispelling the darkness and dismissing fear. The Lord Christ once came here and asked, "Why are you toiling here?" I answered, "I am toiling seeking You, Lord, but You are hiding!" Oh, I cannot bear such happiness!

9 June 1957

Then He said to her, "Your sins are forgiven." And those who sat at the table with Him began to say to themselves, "Who is this who even forgives sins?" Then He said to the woman, "Your faith has saved you. Go in peace." (Luke 9: 48-50)

The blind whinged against the Lord when He said to the sinful woman, who annointed His feet with fragrant oil and wiped them with the hair of her head, 'Your sins are forgiven.' Their disgruntlement was from within their hearts, but He who knows the secrets of the heart. They did not know Him, and so they thought they were righteous in their own eyes. On the other hand, she fully knew Him and that He is the One who saves and gives life, and so she received forgiveness.

When the Lord Jesus knew their thoughts, He did not address them, but rather turned to the sinful woman and spoke to her saying, 'Your faith has saved you.' This was to teach them that faith is the rock that might be shaken, and that anybody that falls on it might bruise, but on whom it might fall, it would crush them.

This was His response to the sinful woman, not only to confirm that her sins were forgiven, but to shine a light on the path for everybody to see. Holy and blessed is He forever.

21 June 1957

The Lord ordered Moses to offer sacrifices of only clean animals, forbidding any unclean animals on His holy altar, so that He could smell the sweet aroma of the offering, and be pleased with humankind. This same thing happened with Noah after the flood. The first thing he did after leaving the ark was to offer a sacrifice to the Lord from among the clean animals. Thus, he deserved to hear God's promise that He would never flood the whole world again.

It is the same with prayer. Our prayers are accepted as a sacrifice and as sweet incense reaching Heaven if they come from a pure heart, but if they are mixed with ungodly thoughts, then we are offering unclean sacrifices on the altar of the Lord. God accepted Abel's sacrifice and rejected Cain's.

3 July 1957

The Presence of God

"And He who sent Me is with Me. The Father has not left Me alone, for I always do those things that please Him." (John 8: 29)

This is what the Lord Jesus said while He was in the treasury, teaching in the temple. We can learn from this that we are continuously present before God, feeling His presence and existence in us and with us. We ought to keep His commandments, and do according to His will, as He dwells in the pure souls and hearts. This is the ultimate, immeasurable joy. How miserable is the life of a solitary monk when he loses the condolences of others, and does not feel any consolance in his own heart. He is then an easy target for the battles of the devil, and there is no helper, because he has not found the pearl of great value.

There must have been a certain object, or sin, which he could not forsake completely, or sell to buy the name of the Lord Jesus, who is highly priced, remembering that "where [our] treasure is, there [our] hearts will be also". How important is the feeling inside a monk that he is in the continuous presence of God, and so a dialogue runs between him and God at all times. Wherever he is, his heart is always praying and repeating the name of our Lord Jesus Christ, asking His forgiveness and guidance, and contemplating His beauty and powerful works. His life becomes consumed with the Lord in everything and in all things, and so he can say "He is with Me, the Father has not left Me alone."

15 July 1957

Our mother the Orthodox Church has strong pure pillars, purified by the blood of the Lord Jesus. The Coptic Orthodox Church believes that Jesus Christ is the Son of the Living God incarnated from the Virgin St Mary through the dwelling of the Holy Spirit in her womb. He came to the world to release us from the slavery of the devil, after the fall of our father Adam and after the death penalty was laid upon him for disobeying God, which resulted in his expulsion from Paradise and his toiling on earth. Therefore all of his descendents became subject to this death penalty, as a result of their father Adam's disobedience.

After 5500 years, the Lord Jesus Christ came to restore Adam, and those souls who had departed, to their original rank. Jesus Christ came to free us all. When He gave up His pure soul on the Cross, Satan came to take His soul, but the strong power and the everlasting Divine Spirit captured and chained him, salvaging those who had been in his grasp since the beginning of time. Those who died in hope waiting for the great day of Salvation and Redemption in order to return to the Heavenly Bosom. The Risen Lord could then say, "I will ransom them from the power of the grave; I will redeem them from death. O Death, I will be your plagues! O Grave, I will be your destruction! Pity is hidden from My eyes" (Hosea 13:14).

This is what Jesus Christ did for us, what then have we done for His sake? O my Lord, we stand in great shame and You are so merciful. Help us to despise this vain life and this perishable body, and to place our souls in Your hands. Do whatever You wish with me, according to Your will. Will you send me to the slaughter, to jail, or to be tortured? I am yours, My Lord, You have purchased me with Your precious blood. I simply ask You to sustain my weak faith. I cannot say my heart is ready my Lord. My heart is not ready, for without You I can do nothing.

Simon Peter dragged a net to land with 153 fish in it, yet the net was not broken (John 21:11). The net is the church, which embraces all her children of all nations. She endures their weaknesses and mistakes, praying for the salvation of all, and that they all come to the knowledge of the truth. She never dismisses a sinner who approaches her in repentance and never forsakes a wicked sinner seeking refuge from the evil world. She is never torn or weakened.

25 July 1957

"For the iniquity of the Amorites is not yet complete" (Gen 15:16).

Often we see the wicked living happily and enjoying life's luxuries, while the children of God are experiencing many temptations. We all know that God is the Almighty just judge. He is only bearing with the sinners until it is their time of judgment and their casting into Hell, thus realising the fruits of their evil deeds and their life away from God.

17 August 1957

"Be faithful unto death, and I will give you the crown of life." (Rev 2: 10)

I have fought the good fight, I have finished the race, I have kept the faith. Finally, there is laid up for me the crown of righteousness." (2 Tim 4:7,8)

As monks we ought to be honest, and honesty requires a lot

of struggle and repentance. We also need to be steadfast, always recalling the early zeal that led us to monasticism. This is something that continues until our last breath, not only for a number of days or years. If a person is given the choice of denying his faith or withdrawing his holy monastery, of course he will offer himself up for slaughter or surrender his body to all kinds of torture, but will not deny his aim in life, "...looking unto Jesus, the author and finisher of our faith." (Heb 12:2).

The issue of honesty is very serious and important in our lives. Through it we achieve our hope of obtaining a strong weapon to fight the traps of the enemy, who is never weary and fights us all the time. We must be honest to the end in our love for the Lord and our neighbour, and be honest in our humility, our illnesses and our tribulations.

Finally we must be very honest during our separation from our Heavenly dwelling unto the last breath.

22 August 1957

"And whatever you ask in My name, that I will do, that the Father may be glorified in the Son." (John 14:13).

We can do everything through our Beloved Jesus Christ. When we ask the Father in the Name of Jesus, who united us with the Father and is the Only Begotten Son, He will provide us with what we ask for. As St Paul teaches us through his Epistles, which are full of grace, "I can do all things through Christ who strengthens me" (Phil 4:13); "In the name of Jesus Christ of Nazareth, rise up and walk'" (Acts 3:6). There are also many other verses proving that there is no other name by which we can be saved except that of the Lord Jesus Christ.

Through Him we were saved from our sins, and by His pure Blood and glorious Resurrection we will enjoy the eternal joy of the Heavenly dwelling. Thus, whoever believes in Jesus Christ has eternal life, and whoever does not will be judged and the wrath of God will fall upon him.

As Christians, we owe a lot to that Great Name. What have we offered to Him who loved us and laid down His life on our behalf? Are we exchanging love with Him? If we could fully comprehend the grace and mercies that Jesus Christ is giving us, we would offer Him our lives, and consider that dying for Him would be appropriate. But how can we do so unless we receive power from Him first? Thus He will be the One working within us and through us for the Glory of His Blessed Name, "If you love Me, keep My commandments. And I will pray the Father, and He will give you another Helper, that He may abide with you forever - the Spirit of truth, whom the world cannot receive, because it neither sees Him nor knows Him; but you know Him, for He dwells with you and will be in you" (John 14:15-17).

7 October 1957

Moses the Prophet ordered the children of Israel to keep the Lord's commandments saying, "And these words which I command you today shall be in your heart. You shall teach them diligently to your children, and shall talk of them when you sit in your house, when you walk by the way, when you lie down, and when you rise up. You shall bind them as a sign on your hand, and they shall be as frontlets between your eyes. You shall write them on the doorposts of your house and on your gates" (Deut 6:6-9).

It is amazing how strict and accurate we must be, even precautious, lest anyone should sin out of negligence or reluctance in fulfilling the Lord's life giving commandments.

Woe to us Christians, and especially the monks, if we fall short of fulfilling our Lord's commandments. The Lord Jesus says that if we break one of these commandments, we break them all. He also says, "You can do nothing without Me." Yes, His commandments are not heavy, but who can be saved if he depends on his own personal struggle alone? We are in great need of the Lord's grace, especially in these spiritually dry times where life is more complicated and evil is increasing. Our enemies, especially the hidden ones, surround us everywhere to trap us while we are unaware. Had it not been for

God's mercies, they would have destroyed us.

So we should always plead, persist and ask for our Heavenly Father's help. He does not wish that any one of us should perish. We must always remember His commandments and depend on Him for their fulfillment, "Jesus answered and said to him, 'If anyone loves Me, he will keep My word; and My Father will love him, and We will come to him and make Our home with him'" (John 14:23). Our aim in life should revolve around loving God and the foundation of our life should be Love.

We worry and are very careful not to upset our Lord if we sin, but how can we keep ourselves from sinning when sin is in our nature? We can do so by keeping His commandments, which in themselves have great power that helps us fulfill them. We have salvation in the great Name of the Lord Jesus Christ, so let us love Him from the depths of our hearts. Whatever we are doing, let our lips speak this Holy Name without ceasing, repeating with St Paul, "For I am persuaded that neither death nor life, nor angels nor principalities nor powers, nor things present nor things to come…can separate us from the love of God" (Rom 8:17) .

He is Holy and Blessed at all times.

20 October 1957

"Woe to you when all men speak well of you, For so did their fathers to the false prophets" (Luke 6:26). The Lord did not mean that we have to commit sin to avoid being praised, but when we fulfill His commandments we will face obstacles. We will have to choose whether to speak and act according to the divine commandment, ignoring those who resist us, or whether we give up the commandment in order to keep our worldly dignity and be praised by others.

The Lord Jesus says, "I do not receive honor from men" (John 5:41). People accused Him of many things: "Now when the Pharisees heard it they said, 'This fellow does not cast out demons except by Beelzebub, the ruler of the demons" (Matt 12:24), and it is the same with the sons of God, the saints, the disciples, the martyrs and the ministers of the Word. They were all persecuted for witnessing for the Truth. St Athanasius was told that the whole world was against him, but he answered that he was against the whole world, because he was sure he was following the way, the truth and the life.

I used to think that this saying contradicted the verse which says, "Let your light so shine before men, that they may see your good works and glorify your Father in heaven"(Matt 5:16), but then my mind was enlightened with this verse, "Woe to you when all men speak well of you, For so did their fathers to the false prophets" (Luke 6:26). The false prophets would tolerate people in their sinful deeds and crooked ways of thinking, depending on their position as prophets, while in reality they were false prophets and their father was the devil, the liar and father of liars. Therefore these false prophets were honoured in the eyes of the people and always received their praise.

In the Old Testament, the same thing happened with Micaiah the Prophet and Ahab the King of Israel, who listened to the false prophets (1 Kings 22).

"A disciple is not above his teacher, nor a servant above his master" (Matt 10:24). The war between what is true and what is false, between light and darkness, purity and impurity, and between what the soul desires and what the body desires will not cease. "But Peter and the other apostles answered and said: 'We ought to obey God rather than men'" (Acts 5:29).

19 November 1957

"And everyone went to his own house, But Jesus went to the Mount of Olives" (John 7:53-8:1). All of the Scribes and Pharisees, those who gathered to judge Jesus, returned to their homes. They returned because they cared only about their bodies, their comfort and their enjoyment of a life of luxury. Their thoughts were worldly and their rest was in a house of clay. They did not know the eternal house built without hands, nor the way that leads to it. They refused to know the way, the truth and life. Shame on them, for they did not know that the day would come when their hypocrisy would be disclosed openly. They returned to their homes to think of new evil tricks to accuse the innocent.

But Jesus went to the Mount of Olives

Jesus went to the Mount of Olives to speak to His Father about the darkness and injustice of humanity, pleading for them to know the way that leads to eternal life. Jesus' resting place is never in houses because, "Jesus said to him, 'Foxes have holes and birds of the air have nests, but the Son of Man has nowhere to lay His head'" (Matt 8:20). Jesus did not go to a house to eat or drink or sleep. He went to the Mount of Olives, where He had another form of food not known by the chiefs of evil. His food was to do the Father's will, which was the salvation of every soul.

Caring for the soul is life, but caring for the body is death. The Chief of Life went to the mountain where there is life for the spirit. Our disturbed soul escapes from the world's troubles and noise into the wilderness where the soul is healed of its illness, and the mind and heart is purified. In the wilderness the spirit is lifted up and becomes sublime through unity with its Creator. After Jesus struggled with the people, He went to the Mount of Olives to continue His spiritual struggle with the Father through prayer, for prayer is the beginning and completion of every good deed.

14 December 1957

"Now there were in the same country shepherds living out in the fields, keeping watch over their flock by night. And behold an angel of the Lord stood before them, and the glory of the Lord shone around them, and they were greatly afraid. Then the angel said to them, 'Do not be afraid, for behold, I bring you good tidings of great joy which will be to all people. For there is born to you this day in the city of David a Savior, who is Christ the Lord'" (Luke 2:8-11).

While the fox Herod was in a deep sleep after indulging in

luxurious desires and while the Scribes and Pharisees were deceiving people, depending on their knowledge and position, here, in the open fields we see the shepherds keeping watch all night, caring for their flock. These poor watchful shepherds were the only ones who deserved to hear the first annunciation about the birth of Jesus, the hope of Israel, whose birth the prophets prophesied hundreds beforehand. The children of Israel were waiting impatiently for the birth of their King and Saviour.

The angel of the Lord appeared to these simple shepherds revealing the good news, comforting them, assuring them not to be afraid but rather to be happy and rejoice because the fullness of time had come. The Saviour of Israel has been born to save His people and illuminate the darkness. What a great joy for those captured in Hades to know that their Saviour was finally coming to save them! "How beautiful on the mountains are the feet of him who brings good news, who proclaims peace, who brings glad tidings, who proclaims salvation…" (Isaiah 52:7).

Simple pure souls like those of the shepherds deserve this grace over others. Blessed are the watchful shepherds because they will give an account for their flock on judgment day. They should never think that they are toiling in vain. Let them take comfort from the shepherds who watched their flocks all night, even though they were in an open area, with no fences to protect them, with enemies around them on every side, and a cloud of witnesses surrounding them.

7 January 1958

Every person should have his share of suffering and tribulations allocated by God. Who can flee from His Face? "Where can I go from Your Spirit? Or where can I flee from Your presence?" (Ps 139:7) Sometimes a person can complain about being in a certain place and think, "If I go somewhere else, I will be happy," but in fact he will find the same or other types of pain wherever he goes. So victory comes from patience, "By your patience possess your souls" (Luke 21:19). Our life on earth is all about falling and rising, "For a righteous man may fall seven times and rise again." (Prov 24:16).

So St Paul the Apostle says, "Do not be haughty, but fear," (Rom 11: 20) because it is written, "conduct yourselves throughout the time of your stay here in fear," (1 Peter 1:17) "redeeming the time, because the days are evil" (Eph 5:16). We need to cling to the Lord Jesus and live with Him in real love and intimacy so that He can be our comforter in tribulations and temptations, and our victory in hardships until we meet Him in heaven. We say this with St Paul, "Yet in all these things we are more than conquerors through Him who loved us" (Rom 8:37).

He is Holy and Blessed at all times.

20 January 1958

"Then they drew near to the village where they were going, and He indicated that He would have gone farther. But they constrained Him, saying, "Abide with us, for it is toward evening, and the day is far spent." And He went in to stay with them. Now it came to pass, as He sat at the table with them, that He took bread, blessed and broke it, and gave it to them. Then their eyes were opened and they knew Him; and He vanished from their sight. And they said to one another, "Did not our heart burn within us while He talked with us on the road, and while He opened the Scriptures to us?" (Luke 24: 28-32)

The Lord appears many times as if He is walking away from us, and we feel a drought in our souls, and we do not usually know that we are the cause, because we did not ask for Him. He yearns to dwell in His house (the soul) because He said, "Behold, I stand at the door and knock. If anyone hears My voice and opens the door, I will come in to him and dine with him, and he with Me" (Rev 3: 20). This teaches us that we ought not to be silent, nor stop purifying our hearts, so that it will be an acceptable upper room for the Lord. Then what happened, "they constrained Him, saying, 'Abide with us'". Here, we do not let go of Him, we cling onto Him like Jacob did when he said, "I will not let You go unless You bless me". We force Him to enter into His new dwelling place, and to purify it according to His good will, for when He enters, He feels the dryness of the soul, and so He fills it with His grace and feeds it with His love. Now it came to pass, as He sat at the table with them, that He took bread, blessed and broke it, and gave it to them. When the soul is fed with His Body and Blood, it becomes drunk with His love, and forgets everything around it. Only then will our hearts eyes be opened, and will the mist of darkness vanish from around the soul, and only then will we begin to feel as if we were in Heaven for "the kingdom of God is within you", and so the soul will receive consolation and will be able to fight and conquer the enemy.

The Holy Fifty Days 1957

The Lord Jesus says, "The wind blows where it wishes, and you hear the sound of it, but cannot tell where it comes from and where it goes." (John 3:8). This is a beautiful simile for the hidden work of the Holy Spirit within human beings.

St James the Apostle says, "My brethren, let not many of you become teachers, knowing that we shall receive a stricter judgment" (James 3:1). This statement corresponds perfectly with the teachings of the early Desert Fathers who lived the life of celibacy and solitude.

Once a novice asked an elder monk what he should do to live as a true honest monk. The elder did not preach or explain Bible verses. He just answered, "Stay in your cell and it will teach you everything." The novice did as he was told and he found great comfort in his spiritual life.

As for this generation in which we are living, with so much technology and knowledge, faith has weakened and consequently, the work of the Spirit has decreased because of the many obstacles resisting its work.

There are so many sermons conducted, thousands of preachers, many educated people, plenty of books and authors, but we find that we are living in a generation which cares for the outer appearance which has very little spiritual depth.

Why do we often deceive ourselves? Why do we care more about the outer appearance than the inner? I am afraid we are the "whitewashed tombs" of which our Lord spoke of. This is happening because we have deviated from the path of our early fathers and are rushing to listen to different teachings, and trying to find a quick fix for our broken souls. We are not giving the Spirit a chance to work within us in tranquility and peace. This only happens when we submit totally to God.

Seal the door of your struggles with silence, lest the tongue destroys it.

The great Saint Isaac taught deep, precious spiritual teachings about silence and serenity and the important role they play in being filled with grace and replacing the old man. He lived during the sixth century and would describe his generation as lukewarm and promiscuous, so what can we say about the generation of the twentieth century? Can we find the kind of silence that St Arsanius described as being able to be broken by the sound of a bird?

4 August 1958

"But as many as received Him, to them He gave the right to become children of God, to those who believe in His name" (John 1:12). What a great honour it is for us as Christians to be called the children of God. This phrase may be said easily and taken for granted, however if we examine it under the strong light of grace, we will realise how precious this honour is. The great Almighty God, the Creator of everything, the unlimited, calls us His children! A father can understand how strong the feeling of love is for his children.

We are the children of God. How awesome and joyful it is to become children, and to know we are no longer slaves. If this is the case, why do we fear tomorrow and what will happen after? The Lord has previously promised us that He will look after us as a Father full of love and kindness, so why worry?

"For God so loved the world that He gave His only begotten Son, that whoever believes in Him should not perish but have everlasting life" (John 3:16) and "See, I have inscribed you on the palms of My hands; Your walls are continually before Me" (Is 49: 16).

He also says that whoever touches you, touches the apple of My eye, and even if a mother forgets her nursing child, I will never forget you.

We trust His promises, so we should be strong in our battle against evil because we are the children of the great King. No matter how grievous our sins are, His mercies are greater, "and my delight was with the sons of men" (Prov 8:31). St Isaac said that He silences the noise of those in heaven in order to listen to the cries and pleas of the human beings who are praying. Let us be strong and steady, and cry out in deep sighs:

O Abba, Father, through our Beloved Saviour Jesus Christ, please do not forget Your creation that You have shaped with Your own Hands. You know our weak nature; we need Your continuous support and help.

6 August 1958

Monks often feel that their spiritual fervour in worship is weakening. This is because we usually use only words, not deeds. For example, a monk might say, "I will start a practice of seclusion, silence, and remaining in my cell," and all kinds of similar practices. If he faces a struggle from the devil or feels boredom, he may fall backward and sink into deep depression, but after so much toil he will be back where he started.

Monasticism is the path to repentance and also the path to death. Our life should be moving forward, not backward. We must be patient until the last breath and when our Lord sees our patience, He will quickly send help and support. Let us leave expressions such as 'spiritual exercises' and 'spiritual retreats' to lay people who are struggling in the world and need spiritual retreats and sessions to revive themselves spiritually. As for us monks, monasticism is a stable continuous way of life, as long as we keep carrying the cross.

Let us continue this until death, following our Master's example.

As a setback occurs in a sick person before he is completely healed, the same happens in us before we are totally free from the old man. For while we are heading forward, we then suddenly fall, giving the evil one a chance to mock and goad us with more fierce fights. We must continue to be patient.

As long as we are still alive we need to be steady in our humility. If we have not completed our service properly, we should wait patiently until we are completely convinced to perform it without doubt or interruption. We should not do this in haste so that we do not fail and become a subject of gloating for our enemies. The proof of this is the strong and stable work of the Spirit within us, "for without Me you can do nothing" (John 15:5).

Monasticism is a ladder on which monks ascend step by step in order to reach perfection, but if they try to jump or skip some steps, they will simply fall to the bottom and so they must be patient, supported by the grace of God, Who tolerates their falls and always endures their weaknesses.

May the Lord have mercy on us all and help us obtain the salvation of our souls.

26 August 1958

There is a hidden battle with the devils because the soul is in pain due to previous sins. If the soul does not completely get rid of the old man, then it will be in conflict with those bad habits, with whom it compromised itself with before, and so will fall into sin as a result.

"Be sober, be vigilant; because your adversary the devil walks about like a roaring lion, seeking whom he may devour" (1 Peter 5:8). Sometimes the soul falls into deep distress and confusion after intense prayer or meditation, as if it is really fighting and struggling with a hidden enemy. But while experiencing this, the soul is depending on the power of faith in its strong tower: Jesus Christ. "The name of the Lord is a strong tower; The righteous run to it and

104

are safe" (Prov 18:10).

In the midst of its fierce struggle, the soul can feel the support of its beloved God whom it is yearning to reach, but which it is prevented from doing so by the guards of darkness. It then feels such peace and comfort and in a blaze of love, therefore it pleads in tears to its beloved Lord Jesus, repeating with the Psalmist "My heart is ready O God," and thus sees all pain as nothing for the sake of this love.

Blessed is the soul that pays its debt willingly while here in the flesh, instead of facing tortures unwillingly in the place where there is no hope and remorse is useless.

The Lord says: "without Me you can do nothing" (John 15:5), also, "'Not by might nor by power, but by My Spirit,' Says the Lord of hosts" (Zac 4:6). So who would dare say that it is because of my courage or piety that I am repenting to face the war with the mighty ones and win salvation? No way! If we are not supported by the Lord's grace, and are not depending on Him or believing in His love, there is no salvation without His Holy Name.

We are so young, our Lord, we do not know the narrow way. We are weak and hopeless, and not as strong as our early fathers who successfully completed their struggle in the blessed call to monasticism. We only depend on your true promise, "Assuredly, I say to you, whoever does not receive the kingdom of God as a little child will by no means enter it" (Mark 10:15). Let us live and stand before you as innocent young children and simple fishermen, hoping to be embraced by Your divine love.

2 October 1958

Then the king said to me, "What do you request?" So I prayed to the God of heaven. And I said to the king, "If it pleases the king, and if your servant has found favor in your sight, I ask that you send me to Judah, to the city of my fathers' tombs, that I may rebuild it." (Nehemiah 2: 4-5)

This is the way the men of God are in life; their lives become continuous with the Lord, they receive help and guidance, and their prayers are heard and answered. They live all their lives in His presence (even though He is near to everybody).

"Then Elijah said, "As the LORD of hosts lives, before whom I stand" and St Paul said: "I was praying to God…", while he was in the middle of a conversation. How much more ought the monks be, who have consecrated their lives to this internal world? How can their souls be liberated from the heaviness of the body, to soar high with Christ and be in His presence forever?

If I do not confirm myself in the truth, until I become an inseperable part of Him, then it does not avail me. For all the honoring I receive from others now, and whatever I enjoy from the lusts of this world will end, either by life or death. And then I look at myself, and I am empty inside. Empty from all consolation, where it comes from true peace. Empty from all the works of grace that girds me in tribulations and wars, the hidden and the manifest. Empty from the continual connection with the true spring that does not run dry, and from where the soul seeks its fruit and is nourished.

And then suddenly I realise that the days and years have passed by and I am still ignorant and I still think I am walking, until I stand in front of the fearful throne of God, and I am naked and in shame and disgrace, and others can see my shame, and where regret is no longer an option. Your mercy O Lord.

17 May 1959

The Lord of glory said to the sinful woman who wiped His feet: "Therefore I say to you, her sins, which are many, are forgiven, for she loved much. But to whom little is forgiven, the same loves little." (Luke 7: 47)

And we know from the teachings of the saints that a person cannot attain the level of true love if they do not first control reverence. But in the story of the sinful woman, we see that the Lord describes her: "for she loved much", whereas when she came to Him, she was in the peak of her sins.

It is truly amazing that our Lord Jesus, our Great Shepherd, who left the ninty nine sheep and went to look for the one lost sheep, who was eating with the sinners and the tax collectors, said that "I did not come to call the righteous, but sinners, to repentance." Therefore, there is no barrier between us and Him, because He yearns towards sinners. Thus there is joy in the presence of the angels of God over one sinner who repents.

And to receive salvation, He looks upon the keeness of the heart and the emotions of love towards Him, which pour out in front of him with silent groaning, silenced by the beastly lusts, overcoming the weak human willpower, which could not find another way to escape from sin.

It is for this reason the Chirst of glory came to our world to break our bonds and to shine in our darkness and heal our souls' pains. We are indebted towards His great Name, without which there would be no salvation.

The first commandment is love, and it is the foundation of all constructions.

Indeed in other spiritual aspects, love is the highest level, and whoever attains it would have attained the top of all other virtues. O great love, full of delicious fruit because you are the pure vine. Draw me closer to the Beloved, so that I may forget my ego and forget my past life, and come under the feet of the Master, to listen to the word of salvation coming out of his blessed mouth; cleansing me from the original man, and granting me everlasting life by offering a pure repentance and through the renewing of the spirit through holiness. Thus in my days of estrangement, my thoughts, hopes, yearnings and emotions are in the Kingdom of Heaven, where my beloved sits amid the praising of the Cherubim and the Seraphim and all the Heavenly Hosts. There I might be counted to participate in the praising and rejoicing without ceasing that does not run dry. Everytime I shout with them, my soul yearns more and my love increases for Him who loved me first. I want to calm down for a little while, but love draws me closer and rekindles in my heart a stronger flame, and thus my soul would continuously be in a relationship with Him.

If I live on earth, my soul belongs up in Heaven. O great love, how magificent and how majestic are you, for God is love.

El Sourian Monastery

23 July 1959

My soul yearned to converse with the spiritually enlightened, and those who have tasted the gifts of the spirit, and to learn from their paths, and how they reached such a spiritual level. How did they transcend and go beyond the realm of this world, and soar high in the heaven of the spirit. How did they knock on the door, and it was happily opened unto them, as they became full in the spirit.

My soul yearns for those who searched diligently to receive the Kingdom of Heaven and its righteousness, who earnestly searched for the hidden treasure inside of them, for their lives are from Him, in Him and to Him they will return. My heart earnestly yearns to be in union with their hearts, to attain the same goal.

There is no doubt that the monastic path needs extensive guidance by a spiritual advisor, and for experience in the same spiritual realm, from someone who has already tried it. Experience about its internal and external warfares, points of weakness, traps set by the devil, and how to overcome them with the weapons of God, among other matters. How accurate is the life of a monk.

1 August 1959

Denying One's Self

"Then Jesus said to His disciples, 'If anyone desires to come after

Me, let him deny himself, and take up his cross, and follow Me. For whoever desires to save his life will lose it, but whoever loses his life for My sake will find it'" (Matt 16:24,25). I can see that monasticism is based on this: denying yourself, carrying the cross and sacrificing your soul (surrender, sacrifice and total death).

It is not easy for a person following the path of virtue and God's commandments to deny himself. How wonderful it is though for a person to achieve this virtue of self denial, for it contains a great degree of humility. How can we deny something that is already existing, being the ego, and let Jesus Christ live within us so that He becomes the one working inside us and with us, for the glory of His holy Name? As for my soul, which has put me in so much trouble, it enjoys the praise of people, leading to its destruction. If it is humiliated or passed over, it becomes angry and envious, and starts to avenge itself…

- The soul that wants to have the biggest share and highest level of praise and compliments does so because of its pride and conceit, while "for he who is least among you all will be great" (Luke 9:47,48).

- It does its best to be famous and well known, and if it can't achieve this openly it puts on a veneer of piety and holiness to gain praise. "Woe to you when all men speak well of you" (Luke 6:26)…"having a form of godliness but denying its power." (2 Tim 3:5)

- Jealousy and envy: If the soul notices that someone else is being praised or honoured, it tries to attract this praise to itself and if it fails, it starts to belittle the praised person in order to attract all eyes to its own fake virtues. When it fails, it envies and feels resentment internally, becoming like a boiling pot.

- The pain of adultery is one of the basic reasons for feeding the ego and is also preceded by pride and haughtiness.

- Murmuring and judging, even audibly, is also a sort of love of the ego. If I consider myself as one who is despised - as said by David the great prophet and king, who was anointed by God but called himself a worm and a dog - then why do I judge others and want to be above everyone else? This is due to a lack of love.

- Also concerning my outer appearance: clothing, walking, sitting amongst other things. Why am I so proud of myself? Why talk about what I have done all the time, as if I am the Creator? Yet I am leading my poor soul to total and permanent darkness…

- What is the remedy for all of these pains inside me? The Lord answers in a simple manner: deny yourself, carry the cross every day, and forget about yourself. It is a matter of denying yourself first, then carrying the cross and forgetting yourself. These are very clear, strong, straight-forward words… (John 12:24)

16 August 1959

"But tarry in the city of Jerusalem until you are endued with power from on high." (Luke 24: 49)

This was the instruction given to the disciples by the Lord before they received the Holy Spirit to go out and preach. For had they been sent to preach but were not given the Holy Spirit, then they would have failed in their preaching. We can apply this verse in our lives for the people who consecrate their lives as monks to live an ascetic life, either by locking themselves up or generally those who are in solitude in a cave in the mountains. They ought to live first in the community of the monks (Konpion), completing the works of obedience and humility under the guidance of an experienced father of confession, to be filled with grace and to train up in virtues until they receive spiritual strength to fend off the devil, and so they would be counted with the victorious in every battle. The Lord will battle for them, and not through their own weak power.

7 December 1959

In the miracle of feeding the five thousand with the five loaves and two fish, there was clear evidence for God's greatness, who was able to work so much through the weakness of many, to make them strong. If His grace creates something out of nothing, then He is able to do absolutely anything. The number ONE is the beginning of all numbers, and a THOUSAND is the completion of numbers, and so are the tens and hundreds. Thus it is written "one day is as a thousand years, and a thousand years as one day".

It is as if the five loaves were enough to feed the five thousand, at the rate of feeding one thousand people with only one loaf. Blessed be our God who is able to feed our hungry souls when He sees the readiness of our hearts, and our struggle to keep all His commandments and to listen to His voice. When our own strengths fail, according to His good will, He gives us grace and feeds and renews our souls. Glory be to God forever.

8 January 1960

"Because the Spirit is truth" (1 John 5: 6)

St John is teaching us that when a person always speaks the truth, senses the truth and lives with truth and in truth, such a person becomes spiritual because he is filled with the Spirit, and the Spirit has started to work through him for the glory of God.

"And you shall know the truth, and the truth shall make you free." (John 8: 32)

If we do not abide in the Spirit, how then can we know the truth?

For this reason we hear Christ talking to Pontius Pilate: "I am a king. For this cause I was born, and for this cause I have come into the world, that I should bear witness to the truth. Everyone who is of the truth hears My voice." Pilate said to Him, "What is truth?"" (John 18: 37-38)

We see that, because Pilate was empty from the spirit, he could not understand the truth, or know it, because he does not believe in Him, therefore whoever is born of the Spirit is spirit, and the man who walks according to the Spirit knows the Spirit, because in Him we live and move and have our being (I am the way, the truth and the life). However, the misleading spirit of this world is Satan, and for this reason Christ said about him that he is a liar and the father of it, and lying is the opposite of truth, "we are in Him who is true, in His Son Jesus Christ. This is the true God and eternal life." (1 John 5: 20)

21 July 1960

"Now when He got into a boat, His disciples followed Him. And suddenly a great tempest arose on the sea, so that the boat was covered with the waves. But He was asleep. Then His disciples came to Him and awoke Him, saying, "Lord, save us! We are perishing!" But He said to them, "Why are you fearful, O you of little faith?" Then He arose and rebuked the winds and the sea, and there was a great calm." (Matt 8: 23-26)

"The Kingdom of God is within you", "you are the temple of God and the Spirit of God dwells in you".

Here we see the remarkable power of our Lord, which requires strong faith, for if we believe that God is dwelling inside of us, then eveyone of us should get inner consolation. No doubt that the Lord is here with us and He fills us from inside, but many a time we go through the same tribulation that the disciples went through here, where the strong waves of tribulation and temptation strikes us, and our strength is quickly drained, and we feel overwhelmed, desperate and alone. At this moment, our faith's eyes are diminished, and we forget that the name of the LORD is a strong tower; the righteous run to it and are safe.

1 August 1960

"He who loves father or mother more than Me is not worthy of Me. And he who loves son or daughter more than Me is not worthy of Me. And he who does not take his cross and follow after Me is not worthy of Me. He who finds his life will lose it, and he who loses his life for My sake will find it." (Matt 10: 37-39)

Monasticism is based upon this foundation. It is great love, which starts off with reverence, and is consumated by love of Christ who loves me and has strengthened my love for Him, and overcame my love for my father, mother, brother, sister and everyone else. Even though I love those people in Christ, but my love to them is not as great as my love to Him, for His love transcends above all hearts and the ability to think or understand.

There are pains and sorrows in the path of love, and just as our beloved Saviour carried the cross and showed His utmost love, thus the servant is not greater than his master. For if He, being righteous, bore pain and suffering for our sakes, how much more ought we to carry our own cross and to die daily for His name's sake.

"Whoever finds his life will lose it." Thus if we do not die to ourselves, we cannot live. What is truly remarkable about the monastic path, is that whatever I desire to do, I should do the exact opposite. If I want to save my body from sickness, I should instead sacrifice my body to keep my soul.

Therefore, monasticism is death to the soul before death to the world. I die, so that Christ may live within me, and what St Paul called 'taking off the old man', and this is not attained except through the gift of God, after being steadfast in the path, until grace visits you. So be patient, O you who struggles.

4 August 1960

"Then the kingdom of heaven shall be likened to ten virgins who took their lamps and went out to meet the bridegroom. Now five of them were wise, and five were foolish. Those who were foolish took their lamps and took no oil with them, but the wise took oil in their vessels with their lamps." (Matt 25: 1-4)

From this we learn that the ten virgins were equal in stature in that they all kept themselves pure and chaste, but the wise ones exceeded the foolish, because they took oil in their vessels, but the foolish ones were content with the oil already in their lamps.

They did not think ahead, that their oil would eventually run out, due to it burning out, and that they would eventually need more oil in case it does run out, so that the lamp may stay lit.

The wise virgins considered this, and it is for this reason that the gospel mentions them by being wise, where wisdom has built its house. The oil in the lamp is the good deeds and pure thoughts that spring forth from a pure heart that is fervent with love towards Christ our Lord. They are constantly ready to meet the Bridegroom, and so they were not content with keeping their virginity, but they constantly cared about fulfilling the commandments, from love and forgiveness to humility, faith, hope and long suffering, and so they were always in constant growth in the love of Jesus, firm in the vine, flowering and bringing forth the fruits of the Spirit, some 30, 60 and a hundred fold.

"But the wise took oil in their vessels with their lamps." Therefore, when the Bridegroom came unexpectedly, they were quick to fill their lamps to be ready to meet the Bridegroom, and so they were considered worthy to enter with Him into the Heavenly wedding.

The Lord made us ready and vigilant to fulfil all the commandments, and not to be content with being just monks, and so letting go of the control of eyes, thoughts and feelings, or failing to subject the body, as it is written, "for whoever shall keep the whole law, and yet stumble in one point, he is guilty of all" (James 2: 10). Let us receive aid from Him, for alone we can do nothing. May His mercy be on us, through the intercessions of St Mary and all His saints. Amen

11 August 1960

"Now behold, two of them were traveling that same day to a village called Emmaus…But their eyes were restrained, so that they did not know Him…Then their eyes were opened and they knew Him; and He vanished from their sight." (Luke 24: 13, 16, 31)

Sometimes it might appear to one who walks in the path of the Lord that he is walking in complete darkness. He wants to see any spiritual scene, or yearn to hear the voice of God to be consoled and encouraged to endure his pains and sufferings, but he walks as if in the dark. He does not realise that the Lord is very close to him. However, He hides Himself for a good purpose. And then suddenly he realises the presence of God only when He allows it. Therefore it is not out of our own personal effort that we feel the Lord, but rather it is the work of grace in the right time, according to His own good will.

18 September 1960

"In the sweat of your face you shall eat bread" (Gen 3: 19)

Blessed be our merciful God. How sweet is the bread of hardships, and how tasteful is the bread obtained after hard work. In so doing, a man fulfils the words of God after he fell, that he has to eat bread in the sweat of his face. It is for this reason that early comfort on earth has nasty and unpleasant effects on its person, both physically and spiritually.

If we apply this matter to a monk who wants to live in solitude, but has not completed the work of the community, most often he will be unstable and nervous.

St Philoxinus explained this matter when he quoted the story of the people of Israel who tasted bitterness and servitude in Egypt as slaves, and then afterwards they were let free in the desert to worship God.

St Paul also mentions the physical and then the spiritual food. Physical food is needed to stay alive, but the Lord Christ called Himself the living Bread which came down from Heaven, for He is the spiritual food, without which we cannot survive spiritually.

We need to attain this spiritual food inside us, and to unite with Him, and to become the dwelling place of God, for without Him we can do nothing. We ought to struggle and fight in the path of repentance, because it is a narrow path. We ought to be patient to save our souls, putting on the new man, so that He might give us our inner food and comfort.

Monday 15 November 1960

"Then the LORD appeared to Solomon by night, and said to him: "I have heard your prayer." (2 Chron 7: 12)

How excellent is it when God hears our prayers. It is the wish of every creature on earth, and it is the end of the struggle of every struggler who seeks perfection, and it is also a sure sign of the love between a son and his father, who walks according to his will.

How can a monk attain this level, of having his prayers heard by the Lord. To my knowledge, it is impossible, unless he fulfils the commandments of the Lord, because the effective, fervent prayer of a righteous man avails much. How can we be righteous, if we are sinners and have no righteousness within us. Yes, we can do all things through Christ who strengthens us, because He is our righteousness and He completes our weaknesses. For this reason we ought to be attached to Him until the very end, to be confirmed in Him and Him in us, and thus we can bring forth fruit of the spirit. This will happen if we remain steadfast in the vine, otherwise we will wither away and be cut off.

However, how to pray is a great matter, because not every man who stands and recites a few words has prayed, but indeed prayer has many paths, and different exercises, limitations and qualities, because it is the food of the soul and it is also a gift of the Spirit. Let us ask God to grant us true spiritual prayer, which is heard by Him, and not only heard, but also answered, according to His good will.

God hears all the groans of the soul, before He hears our words. He examines our depth, and knows all things.

If we want our prayers to be heard and answered, it is truly a marvelous thing.

Elijah was a man with a nature like ours, and he prayed earnestly that it would not rain; and it did not rain.

I pray that I have the ability to keep writing about this topic, but the beginning and the end are in His hands.

May He be blessed forever, forgiving our sins, and hearing our pleadings.

31 December 1960

"But the ones that fell on the good ground are those who, having heard the word with a noble and good heart, keep it and bear fruit with patience." (Luke 8: 15)

Our Lord spoke about the virtue of patience, for every action and every struggle, if it is not crowned with patience, avails nothing.

"By your patience possess your souls"

What is the benefit if I begin to do a good deed, but am stopped by an obstacle or through the temptation of the devil, and I stop doing this good deed? I have lost my goal, and thus have failed to complete the good deed.

If we contemplate on the struggle of our forefathers the monks, we see that they tasted the bitterness at the start, and tribulations persisted with them, along with the temptations of the devil, for years. In the end, we hear their testimony that they received comfort and inner peace. This comfort and peace is a state of renewal of the Holy Spirit of their hearts, working in might and strength to confirm them, as in the day they received the Holy Spirit in Baptism.

We, the Christians, have received the gift of renewal of our old man in the Holy Baptism, and through the Confirmation of the Mayroon, but when we walk in the world, our flesh is tempted by the lusts of the flesh and the pride of life overwhelms us. Above all of this, the envy of our enemy does not stop or cease to tempt us, and set traps for us to deceive us and drag us away, so that everyone has received the punishment of resisting God Himself.

Instead of being temples for His Holy Spirit, to dwell in our hearts, we willingly accepted to deviate and resist God's work in our hearts, and the Holy Spirit who we received in the day of Baptism. We accepted to be led by the devil to live in sin and to do according to the will of the evil one.

"When a strong man, fully armed, guards his own palace, his goods are in peace. But when a stronger than he comes upon him and overcomes him, he takes from him all his armor in which he trusted, and divides his spoils." (Luke 11: 21-22)

If we want to defeat this mighty enemy, which is sin, we ought to uproot it and cast it out of our hearts, and to prepare our souls to return to its correct use, which is to be the dwelling place of the Spirit of God, and to bring forth fruit of the fruits of the Spirit which love, joy, peace, long-suffering, kindness, goodness, faithfullnes, gentleness and self-control. (Gal 5:22)

It is for this sole reason that monasticism arose, and was founded on this principle – the principle of repentance. Our forefathers built their spiritual life on this strong foundation; for monasticism is death – with all the meaning of the word – and for a monk to reach the state of renewal, he needs to be patient for his whole life, and therefore patience becomes the most important virtue to remain steadfast and to bring forth fruit, and later to receive the eternal life, as without holiness no one will see the Lord. Glory be to God forever.

16 September 1961

True Christians

"Not everyone who says to Me, 'Lord, Lord,' shall enter the kingdom of heaven, but he who does the will of My Father in heaven" (Matt 7:21). Our
Lord Jesus Christ teaches us that it is not enough to repeat words,

many or few, such as, "Lord, Lord". I can also say that even perpetual prayers are not sufficient to enter into the Kingdom of Heaven. In saying this I am not belittling prayer, which is our shield and our source of strength and support, however there is danger in becoming accustomed to repeating our prayers just to complete an order. The Lord came and was incarnated to teach us important things, so we can enter His Kingdom by His great mercy and not because of any goodness within ourselves, "The thief does not come except to steal, and to kill, and to destroy. I have come that they may have life and that they may have it more abundantly" (John 10:10).

The Lord taught us His holy commandments and taught us that they are not heavy. Though we have to enter through the narrow gate and go through many hardships and tribulations, when compared to the apparent pleasure of sin that leads to total destruction on earth and eternal condemnation.

If we consider all of the sufferings of our saintly fathers, we will see that they witnessed for the Lord in many different ways, each according to his spiritual stature. Thus they forgot their pains and felt joy, even during their suffering, for the sake of the Beloved One. It is clear that as Christians we are not of this world, for if we were then we would be submissive to the chief of this world and comforted by his material things that pass away. On the contrary, we are the children of Light, surrendering in joy to our Heavenly King, our Lord Jesus Christ who purchased us with His precious blood. We must act in a manner that pleases Him in this life, fulfills His will from the depth of our hearts, depends on His power, and asks for His support. For without Him we can do nothing.

25 January 1962

"But remember me when it is well with you, and please show kindness to me; make mention of me to Pharaoh, and get me out of this house." (Gen 40: 14)

When Joseph was in prison, and he interpreted the dream of the butler, he asked him "remember me when it is well with you, and please show kindness to me; make mention of me to Pharaoh, and get me out of this house." And indeed the dream was fulfilled and the butler went back to his position, and the Bible mentions "Yet the chief butler did not remember Joseph, but forgot him".

This happens with us frequently. We forget the good deeds and mercies of our Lord, which He treats us with, and when we are in a hardship our prayers increase dramatically, and we vow and pray fervently for God to deliver us from this hardship.

And when God bestows upon us with relief, we forget everything. We are taken away by our worries about the world and pride of life, and we forget what we vowed to God and others.

For this reason, St Paul taught us, saying: "but exhort one another daily, while it is called "Today," lest any of you be hardened through the deceitfulness of sin" (Heb 3: 13).

How often does man forget good gifts! We always need to remind ourselves that we are indebted to God for His unimaginable love towards us, and His gentle association with us, as He did not judge us according to our sins, but instead has showerd us with immense grace.

We are also in debt to our Christian brothers, because what God has bestowed upon me, whether gifts, money, work or blessings is not for me, but rather is a treasure of goodness which He has made me ruler over to distribute to others. For out of His goodness we shall give Him back.

We can contemplate on this story from Joseph's side as well. What does he say: "For indeed I was stolen away from the land of the Hebrews; and also I have done nothing here that they should put me into the dungeon".

The planning of God is truly marvelous and wonderful, for He exalts whom He wants, and puts down whom He wants. He lifts the needy out of the ash heap, so He may seat him with princes and He has put down the mighty from their thrones, and exalted the lowly.

God has chosen people everywhere, and He knows them and He tests them with the fire of tribulations to purify and exalt them, to prepare them for a certain job. The Holy Bible is full of examples of prophets, apostles and saints. These people experienced very dark days, to the point that they thought they had ceased to exist, and yet the eye of the Lord was merciful and His mercy kept them alive, even in the midst of a fiery furnace, or with vicious lions, or in seas or prisons.

Joseph was innocent, sold by his own brothers. He could have told those who bought him that it was his own brothers that sold him, and maybe he would have been saved. Yet he did not, but he totally relied on the valiant hand of the Lord, and he left matters in His hands.

He was sold as a slave, and served Potiphar with all honesty. He was tempted with the harshest temptation faced by any youth. It was so harsh because it was persistent, day after day. But because he was hiding in the stronghold of the Lord, keen to complete the commandment of the Lord, His commandment protected him from falling in sin, whose fallen are all of great stature and whose injured are many.

In the end, his reward was being thrown in jail unfairly. He could have defended himself from this false accusation, but he did not. It is as if he wanted to drink the cup of suffering until drunkenness, like his Lord our Christ. During all of this, no miracle occurred from Heaven to get him out of jail, and yet he was patient for the heavenly verdict.

"But even if you should suffer for righteousness' sake, you are blessed", and this happened because his heart was filled with divine peace, which is the reason for fulfilling the commandments of the Lord. Even when he was in prison, he felt deep peace because the Lord was with him. In contrast, the evil person does not have peace within him, and so even if they are on thrones with great people, they will not have peace.

We see the inevitable result of such patience and endurance, that God took him out of prison and raised him and made him ruler over all of the land of Egypt, and he was the reason for the survival of thousands of people, including his own father and brothers.

How great, then, is the virtue of patience, enduring the pain and suffering of temptations and tribulations that attack us from both human beings and from Satan, as well as the pains of the person themselves! As long as the person persists and struggles, and does not give up, then God will allow the day to come when all these pains and struggles are healed, and He will unbind us from the bonds of sin from Satan, and will mortify our sinful desires. Thus we will feel that we are taken out of prison and are able, through the grace of God, to bring forth eternal fruit, and a great inheritance with those who loved Him and have pleased Him with their good conduct, and through acts of mercy and compassion. Glory be to God forever. Amen

19 February 1962

"Then the priests, the Levites, arose and blessed the people, and their voice was heard; and their prayer came up to His holy dwelling place, to heaven" (2 Chron 30: 27)

"Your prayers and your alms have come up for a memorial before God." (Acts 10: 4)

"Cornelius, your prayer has been heard, and your alms are remembered in the sight of God" (Acts 10: 31)

"Thus says the LORD, the God of David your father: "I have heard your prayer, I have seen your tears" (Isa 38: 5)

"I have surely seen the oppression of My people … and have heard their cry … Now therefore, behold, the cry of the children of Israel has come to Me." (Exo 3: 7-9)

How beautiful is it when our prayers are heard before the Lord, and our prayers enter His dwelling place! This is the desire of those who love Him with all their hearts, who struggle all their lives to fulfil all His commandments to live in His sight in straightness of heart and purity of the soul, until He looks down upon them and hears their cries, and unbinds them from the bonds of the devil, both hidden and manifest. Then they will praise Him continuously in joy and delight. This will allow them to ask and they shall be heard in the day of their trouble, and so He will come and save those who trust in Him.

Blessed is our beloved Lord Jesus who saves our souls, and who humbled Himself to come into our world to save us and unite us with Him.

Now I ask myself, are my prayers heard in His dwelling place? Or has it become a routine? And if so, then what are the ways to purify my prayers to be acceptable before Him? To my knowledge, nothing pleases God more than to see the purity of the heart of man, for it is the source of life for the body, and it is also a spiritual spring bringing forth life to feed the soul. Therefore man ought not to say I am a layman, or a monk, or a priest or a bishop. God does not look at the outer appearance like we do, but He examines the heart and knows the intentions. If priesthood is the promoted and elect people before God in church, then monasticism is consecration of the whole life to God.

I fear that, having been called a monk and priest, I would become a stumbling block to others. People might think more of me than what they can see, when God sees everything inside of me, and might have a different judgement of my character.

St Isaac the Syrian said that work saves a man, regardless of its shape or name.

Therefore, let us pay attention to purifying our hearts and souls from the pains of the original man, and through the grace of God, may we be renewed by the work of the Holy Spirit, who gave strength to the disciples on the day of Pentecost. May our souls become the dwelling place for Him, who makes intercession for us with groanings, which cannot be uttered, remembering the verse "You are the temple of God and that the Spirit of God dwells in you", may our prayers ascend to heaven as sweet aroma to the dwelling place of the most High God. And may the Lord accept us to Him, and hear our prayers, and may He be the subject of our joy and delight.

But be aware, lest we fall to the commandments of man, and stumble in fulfilling the commandment of our Lord. Let us be alert, for many have lost their path in making the means as a goal... "to the Jews a stumbling block and to the Greeks foolishness".

May the Lord protect us from the right hand blows, because the path of simplicity is a sure path.

Glory be to God forever

Sunday 4 March 1962

"Therefore be patient, brethren, until the coming of the Lord. See how the farmer waits for the precious fruit of the earth, waiting patiently for it until it receives the early and latter rain. You also be patient. Establish your hearts, for the coming of the Lord is at hand." (James 5: 7-8)

A monk struggles from the very beginning, in fastings and vigils, prayers and prostrations, humility and obedience and in serving the community of monks, in solitude and isolation, and he begins to long for the presence of the Lord to fill him with consolation and grace, and he awaits the divine gifts, which he has read about in the books of saints such as St Isaac the Syrian or St John Saba.

He yearns for the higher spiritual levels, which he has heard of, and all of this in a few years. He expects to reap the fruit before the seed dies in the ground.

Poor is this man, if he is a layman struggling in the path of the Spirit in the world, or if he is a monk who seeks solitude and serenity.

We hear the words of St James, "be patient" which is a beautiful word, which requires a lot of deep contemplations, because great are the mistakes of wanting to rush things in the path of the Lord, and so He teaches us to be patient. The incarnation of the Word, and His coming into our world is a great example of patience, because He was patient for five thousand years before He perfected the plan of salvation. If we rush, and we ask for something that is not in its right time, it becomes a transgression against the divine plan of God, because we might be asking for something at the wrong time, which might be harmful to us.

But God, who does exceedingly abundantly above all that we ask or think, knows what is best for us, and He gives us in the right time as it pleases Him, who stretches out His hands to feed all living creatures. "See how the farmer waits for the precious fruit of the earth, waiting patiently for it until it receives the early and latter rain." This is true in the science of vegetation, because a fruit that develops too early is weak and is worthless. St Isaac the Syrian said, "every gift that comes without effort, consider it as a still born child, that has no life in it". The quicker it comes, the quicker it goes away. Therefore, remain steadfast in hearts and know that the coming of the Lord is close.

It is very important that we remain steadfast in keeping the commandments of the Lord, and to love Him with all the heart above all things, not looking forward to His gifts and rewards, otherwise our love will be for a hidden purpose. These gifts come naturally; and He is honest in His promises, for when the heart is purified, the gifts come of their own accord naturally; just as a magnet attracts a metal piece, thus the soul that awaits the coming of the Bridegroom and His dwelling in it. Let us remain steadfast in Christ, wherever we are, and however we are, whether we are in the darkness of the soul, or in boredom and weariness, and even if we have no consolation in any shape or form. Our Lord is merciful, for He shines from time to time in the soul of His beloved ones. These visitations are a testimony of His love to the devout and honest soul, until the time comes when He will come and dwell in the heart, and then the person will feel like he was taken up to heaven, even while his body is still on earth. This is the renewal of the Holy Spirit.

This comes after a long time of struggle, battles and tribulations, which test the honesty and love of those who seek the Lord with great hope. Everything is given according to His will and through the divine grace.

"Every good gift and every perfect gift is from above, and comes down from the Father of lights, with whom there is no variation or shadow of turning." (James 1: 17)

19 March 1962

"Manasseh was twelve years old when he became king, and he reigned fifty-five years in Jerusalem. But he did evil in the sight of the LORD, according to the abominations of the nations whom the LORD had cast out before the children of Israel. For he rebuilt the high places ... he raised up altars for the Baals, and made wooden images; and he worshiped all the host of heaven and served them. He also built altars in the house of the LORD...And he built altars for all the host of ... he caused his sons to pass through the ... he practiced soothsaying, used witchcraft and sorcery, and consulted mediums and spiritists. He did much evil in the sight of the LORD, to provoke Him to anger. He even set a carved image ...So Manasseh seduced Judah and the inhabitants of Jerusalem to do more evil than the nations ... And the LORD spoke to Manasseh and his people, but they would not listen...Now when he was in affliction, he implored the LORD his God, and humbled himself greatly before the God of his fathers, and prayed to Him; and He received his entreaty, heard his supplication, and brought him back to Jerusalem into his kingdom. Then Manasseh knew that the LORD was God... and commanded Judah to serve the LORD God of Israel." (2 Chron 33: 1-16)

Holy is our gracious God, and patient on the sinners, for He desires all men to be saved and to come to the knowledge of the truth. We see in this story how Manasseh sinned greatly against God, and defiled the House of God, and submitted to the will of the devil blindly, as the Holy Bible says about him: "he practiced soothsaying, used witchcraft and sorcery, and consulted mediums and spiritists. He did much evil in the sight of the LORD, to provoke Him to anger." Thus he brought with him thousands of people to sin against God.

He truly lost the way, and was difficult to be saved. However, in the life of King Manasseh, the power of repentance and humility is beheld, and the fact that tribulations are allowed by God to alert His sons who have strayed away, to be vigilant and to return to God with repentance, for their sins to be forgiven and wiped away. That they may return to the stronghold of God, fleeing from the evil one who has bound them with iron fetters to strip them away from the grace of God. When they are unbound, they would offer true repentance and remorse for their past sins, with a broken heart, to receive salvation.

Repentance brings forth sons who are renewed, and tribulations alert the slumbered souls, so welcome the tribulations sent by our caring and merciful God, for the rod of a gentle father on his son is to teach him, but is gentle not to kill him, and as David the Psalmist says: "Try my mind and my heart."

The sins of King Manasseh were too many to list, which exceeded all levels of sin, and it did not just stop at him, but extended to the people of Israel, he "seduced Judah and the inhabitants of Jerusalem to do more evil than the nations", and the Bible mentions that whoever makes one of these little one stumble, it would be better for him if a millstone were hung around his neck, and he were drowned in the depth of the sea. How much more does Manasseh deserve, then?!

"Therefore the LORD brought upon them the captains of the army of the king of Assyria, who took Manasseh with hooks, bound him with bronze fetters, and carried him off to Babylon. Now when he was in affliction, he implored the LORD his God."

He was lost in darkness and the enemy had hardened his heart against his Lord, and Manasseh insisted in provoking God. However, God was patient on him. He was able to wipe him away in a moment of time, but He waited to make Manasseh an example to all generations, to show His servants that He opens His arms wide open to accept all sinners who return to Him with repentance.

We knew from His Gospels that He is merciful and patient beyond all understanding, "a bruised reed He will not break, and smoking flax He will not quench". When the sinful woman was caught in the act, and was brought to Jesus to condemn her, what did Jesus say? "He who is without sin among you, let him throw a stone at her first". When everyone was heavy burdened with their own sins, nobody could cast the first stone, and so one by one they began to leave, fearing that their sins may be made public.

Jesus said to the woman, "Woman, where are those accusers of yours? Has no one condemned you? She said, "No one, Lord." And Jesus said to her, "Neither do I condemn you; go and sin no more."

Thus, He teaches us that His mercy and patience on sinners is to allow them to repentance.

Our merciful Lord knows our human weakness and that we are normally inclined to sin and evil, and so He set the path of repentance for us to reach Him. Beware of lingering too long away from the right path, because He said if you fall, then rise again, and He is waiting at the door knocking, and when He sees us coming to Him from a far distance He runs towards us to receive us and accept us back to Him. He would then clothe us with a new garment, because we were dead and now we are alive, and we were lost and now have been found. Heaven rejoices at the repentance of one sinner.

20 March 1962

"You shall love the LORD your God with all your heart, with all your soul, with all your strength, and with all your mind." (Luke 10: 27)

If we love God from all our hearts, souls, and strength, then how can we love Him with all our minds?

I think that our Lord Christ meant that we should gradually increase our love for Him, until we reach the love from all the mind. This is the highest level, and saints and hermits lived in this stage where they would live in the joy of the Lord in their waking hours, during sleep, when eating, during work and when walking.

This is what the fathers meant by the expression 'controlling the mind'. They attained this level after living for long years in great struggle with their own nature, and with devils. They struggled until the blood and death, with the enemy who wants to separate man from his Creator.

This is the degree of completeness, which they refer to as 'crucifying the mind'. They told us, regarding it, 'whoever is crucified has accepted purging of the sins of the original man, and from the wrath of God which was destined for him.' Thus they were indeed correct.

128

There is no doubt that there is a risk in controlling the mind in such a manner, for a person who lives in the world, or for a monk living in the monastery, if they have no proper guidance from someone who is more experienced in this struggle, and who has been given grace.

When a student asked his teacher about continual prayer, he replied, "rejoice, my brother, that continual prayer is reached by those who have reached a state of completeness, through which they can appreciate its value. It will come of its own accord, because it is written, 'the Spirit Himself makes intercession for us with groanings which cannot be uttered.'"

St Paul also teaches us, "bringing every thought into captivity to the obedience of Christ," (2 Cor 10: 5) and I think he means that we ought to cast out every evil thought that does not agree with the commandment of the Lord. This implies that we ought to have the commandments before us as a mirror to measure up to the will of the Lord.

We should, therefore, begin by saying that we should love God from all the mind, if the only thought and the strongest thought is the love of God, which dominates all other thoughts. And we can stop here.

However, if we explain the meaning of the love of God from all the mind literally, then we ought to add continual prayer, which we mentioned earlier. Continual prayer must be followed by 'crucifying the mind' always before the Lord, which we have not yet received from the grace of God. How can I love God without praying to Him, because prayer and reiteration are the bonds of divine love! I think that this level would not be given to a person who is always worried about materialistic things, nor to a beginner monk. However, as St John the Short said, "the baskets are for the camel, the baskets are for the camel" because his mind was subdued by God, that he forgot what the man asked of him.

25 March 1962

"The LORD is with you while you are with Him. If you seek Him, He will be found by you; but if you forsake Him, He will forsake you." (2 Chron 15: 2)

"Because you have forsaken the LORD, He also has forsaken you." (2 Chron 24: 20)

The Lord sent Shemaiah the prophet to Rehoboam and to the leaders of Judah and said to them, "You have forsaken Me, and therefore I also have left you in the hand of Shishak "(2 Chron 12: 5) and thus we see that the Lord is honest in His word, that He will be with us as long as we seek Him, but if we neglect His commandment, then He will deliver us into the hands of the enemy, for a while, to realise that we can do nothing of our own, because in Him we live and move and have our being.

When we feel that we are distant from Him, and we feel the power of temptation, and that we can do nothing on our own without Him, we cry out with Jonah the prophet from the belly of the fish. Since the Lord is near, and He examines our depths, "For the eyes of the LORD run to and fro throughout the whole earth, to show Himself strong on behalf of those whose heart is loyal to Him" (2 Chron 16:9), He hears our cries and listens to our groans, He sees our tears and He comes down and delivers us in various ways. He delights our hearts and comforts our souls, until we receive peace that we have lost, and reconcile with our great God with the covenant of repentace and returning to him. The more we humble ourselves to eat from the pods of the pigs, which does not fill our hunger, we will realise that we belong to Him as His sons and daughters.

We learn a valuable lesson for the future; that we ought to ask for assistance and to be in continual vigil from the traps of the enemy towards our weak nature and our inclination to sin. We ought to remain steadfast in Him, holding on to Him, as we enter with Him into our hearts, and to dine with Him.

Our souls would be comforted and His love will mesmerise us, so that we are in continual communication with him, whether we are sleeping or are awake. We say to Him, "I am my beloved's, and my beloved is mine. He feeds his flock among the lilies." Thus, if we eat or drink, we are alive with Him forever. Glory be to God forever.

29 October 1963

Fruit of Virtue

"The righteous shall flourish like a palm tree, He shall grow like a cedar in Lebanon. Those who are planted in the house of the Lord shall flourish in the courts of our God. They shall still bear fruit in old age; They shall be fresh and flourishing" (Ps 92:12-14).

Saint Isaac the Syrian says, "Know my son that silence, meaning solitude, and any other virtue gives fruit according to our persistence and patience in practicing it." Continuous work, even if it is small, will bear plenty of fruit in the long run. We are often mistaken in thinking that the path of holiness and the proper spiritual life is a short, easy one and that acquiring more virtues depends on our own righteousness. We think that becoming saints can happen by just imitating the lives of saints… This will actually lead to a life that is spiritual in appearance but not a genuine one. In doing this, we will be completely deceiving ourselves, and after some years, we will lose our initial spiritual warmth and return to lukewarmness. We realise that the flame which we thought was igniting us has been put out, thus resembling the fig tree that had many leaves but no fruit. The Lord Jesus is asking for the fruits of the Spirit within our souls, not just the outer appearance of worship. We should be aware of this so that we do not become like the cursed fig tree.

Abba Agathon was once asked, "Which is the greater, our bodily toil or guarding what is inside?" He answered, "A person resembles a tree: the toil of the body is the leaves but guarding what is inside is the fruit. So, each tree that does not bear fruit will be cut and cast away in the fire." Let us preserve the fruit by preserving our thoughts. We need the leaves to cover, protect and decorate the fruit. I really like the saying by an elder who said, "If you see a youth ascending to heaven according to his desires, pull him down by the feet, because this is more beneficial for him."

We cannot just imitate those who struggled and won, because we do not know the full details of their struggles, their wars with the devils, their falls, their victories, etc., for it is impossible for all of the details of their experiences to have been recorded.

The saints were all ornamented with a very important virtue by which they conquered, that is patience, as it is written, "By your patience possess your souls" (Luke 21:19). The saints bore fruits through their patience. The continuous dripping of water on a rock will make a hole in the rock and so, by patience you can accomplish a great task. Nature which surrounds us is a great teacher of patience, for each thing takes time to grow and become mature, as the Lord mentions in the parable of the mustard seed and how it grows (Mark 4:28). The same goes for the children of God who love and worship Him in Spirit and truth, and withstand all things in patience for His sake. They depend totally on Him when facing temptation or a war from the devil. They are the ones whose spiritual growth progresses in a calm, natural manner, without excessive advances or deviations.

Now we have learned that spiritual gifts and fruits are the result of a long period of true worship and the love of God fulfilling His commandments.

16 May 1966

"So it was, when Ahab heard those words, that he tore his clothes and put sackcloth on his body, and fasted and lay in sackcloth, and went about mourning. And the word of the LORD came to Elijah the Tishbite, saying, "See how Ahab has humbled himself before Me? Because he has humbled himself before Me, I will not bring the calamity in his days. In the days of his son I will bring the calamity on his house." (1 Kings 21: 27-29)

This story expresses to us the strength of repentance, and the vast greatness of God's tenderness on His own creation, and that He does not wish death for the sinner, but rather that he may repent and live. And as the common saying says: "we will not be judged for sinning, but rather that we did not repent."

For our life in this flesh, and in this evil world, is constantly

132

under scrutiny and we are always prone to sinning, due to our sinful nature and so it is crucial that we repent daily on our beds of all the sins that we commited during the day.

Blessed is the soul that repents, and is always ready to meet its Heavenly Bridegroom. Also, God is so merciful and patient and He is willing to accept anyone who comes to Him. It is said about Ahab: "But there was no one like Ahab who sold himself to do wickedness in the sight of the LORD" (1 Kins 21: 25).

15 June 1966

The Struggle of a Monk!

It is easy for a person who is struggling to reach perfection to convince himself that he is fulfilling the commandments because he cares more about the outer appearance of his worship than the inner state of the heart. But as for a monk's struggle, he cares about pulling out the pains in his soul by the roots and lives totally with God, without any hurdles or obstacles. In order to reach perfection in Jesus Christ, a monk must love God with all his heart, mind, soul and might and guard his thoughts, for they are the gateway for sin. So he becomes like a soldier carrying his weapon, ready to fight and dismiss the enemy at all times. He never negotiates any thought with the enemy because to do so is to entertain that thought. A monk must remain continually vigilant lest the enemy steal his possessions. I think when the Lord says that we should not sleep; he did not mean the natural rest of the body, because this is a must for human beings. He meant spiritual vigilance, that is, being aware of the enemy and his tricks, because while people are 'sleeping,' the enemy comes and plants his weeds, as mentioned in the Holy Bible. May the Lord grant me a life of watchfulness and help me, for the sake of the salvation of my soul.

20 July 1966

"And everyone who has left houses or brothers or sisters or father or mother or wife or children or lands, for My name's sake, shall receive a hundredfold, and inherit eternal life. But many who are first will be last, and the last first." (Matt 19: 29-30)

"And when those came who were hired about the eleventh hour, they each received a denarius…Is it not lawful for me to do what I wish with my own things…So the last will be first, and the first last. For many are called, but few chosen." (Matt 20: 9-16)

The first set of verses indicates the calling of monasticism, where a monk leaves all his belongings, without any association with anybody, in worship and love with Christ his Lord. He struggles to grow in virtues and in the knowledge of our Lord, and God multiplies His spiritual gifts in this life and makes him inherit eternal life also. However, if he does not remain steadfast till the end, then he will lose everything. If he starts his spiritual life correctly, but then loses enthusiasm and spiritual growth, then he will be delayed, and maybe someone else who came after him would exceed him in spiritual struggle, and inherit eternal life before him.

The second set of verses indicates the serving in the field of the Lord, which are preaching and proclaiming the word of the Lord.

Even though these two sides differ in the way they reach Heaven, but the Lord ends them with the same condition, which is to remain steadfast and in continual growth whilst avoiding slowing down, as He says that God who began with us a good deed, is able to complete it until the end, and the Lord is with us as long as we are with Him, but if we forsake Him, He will forsake us, but He remains honest in His promises, and truthful to those who do His commandments. Let us ask God to assist us in all our struggles.

"Many who are first will be last, and the last first"

24 October 1966

"Launch out into the deep and let down your nets for a catch." (Luke 5: 4)

Our Lord Christ teaches us how a faithful servant can catch souls, and return them to the pasture of salvation. We can also apply this to the monastic path, and to those who walk the path of repentance. Thus it applies to those who worship God in Spirit and truth, and who deepen their love for God. They shall never be shaken by the forces of evil, or the temptations of life, however strong they may be.

We ought to deepen our relationship with the Spring of Life, Jesus Christ, and grow in the knowledge of His love, completing all His commandments in diligence and enthusiasm, until we say with St Paul, "it is no longer I who live, but Christ lives in me" (Gal 2: 20).

Let us beware of vain glory, which is the pest to every virtue, and it destroys the tower of righteousness. Let us enjoy the mocking and ridicule of others, and whatever the devil brings our way to stumble our footsteps, and let us not entertain any thoughts of vain glory. It is not enough to reject it verbally, but we must also exclude it from our souls, even if we do not respond by words to those who praise us, remembering our own sins and mistakes in the past and the present, and also to remember the thought "if the righteous one is scarcely saved, where shall I the sinner appear".

Feast of ascension 30 May 1968

"You have become estranged from Christ, you who attempt to be justified by law; you have fallen from grace. For we through the Spirit eagerly wait for the hope of righteousness by faith." (Gal 5: 4-5)

St Paul teaches us that regardless of our works and struggles, they cannot justify us. This does not mean that we should forsake struggling, but that we should not rely on our own righteousness. But rather it is through faith, which strengthens the hope in us and makes us worthy to receive the suffering of our Saviour, who humbled Himself for our sake, and has redeemed us through His Blood, that we are justified. We are saved through relying on His love and guidance, and His truthful promises, because all our struggles are as the dust of the earth. May the Lord have mercy on us.

15 August 1968

Let us examine what St Paul said, "if anyone should boast, let them boast in the Lord". Sometimes a person will forget himself and start to talk about himself in matters pertaining to teaching others about his own life that praises the Lord, and in doing so he is asking for the praise of the listeners. This sends the message to the listener that the speaker is either boasting in himself, or that he is asking for glory to be attributed to him. However, we hear of saints who would sit together and discuss the glory of God. They wanted to express the glory of God in their lives, and that without Him, they can do nothing. They have been given grace in earthen vessels, that the excellence of the power may be of God and not of us, so that we may be encouraged to remain steadfast in the struggle in the work of God. In either case, the intention of the speaker is not to attract the praise of the listener, not even mentally, so that if he hears someone praising him, he would be delighted, or be pleased when hearing the praise of others to him in his own mind. He is able to do so by remembering his past mistakes and sins, and how God protected and covered him, and did not expose it to the listeners. These verses should express this meaning more clearly:

"Not walking in craftiness nor handling the word of God deceitfully, but by manifestation of the truth commending ourselves to every man's conscience in the sight of God ... For we do not preach ourselves, but Christ Jesus the Lord, and ourselves your bondservants for Jesus' sake... who has shone in our hearts to give the light of the knowledge of the glory of... we have this treasure in earthen vessels, that the excellence of the power may be of God and not of us." (2 Cor 4: 1-7)

If this principle is unacceptable to many, and especially to beginners, then at least the speaker should have the intention of killing their own ego to glorify God in every word or deed, for in Him and by Him all things are, and in Him we live and move and have our being.

21 February 1970

"So He Himself often withdrew into the wilderness and prayed" (Luke 5:16).

Our Lord Jesus Christ teaches us how to pray a strong, fruitful and acceptable prayer when we are praying privately, away from anyone or any worldly concern. This cannot be achieved without fleeing to the wilderness. Perhaps the wilderness here means the heart, as the real wilderness has now been settled and filled with buildings, and even the Lord said enter into your bedroom, that is, the heart, and pray to your Father who is in Heaven. The heart should be rid of any other concerns in order to relate to God without hindrance. There is no doubt that the serenity of the wilderness has the great effect of emptying the heart of all concerns and helping it to soar like an eagle, without any worldly burdens that weigh it down or prevent it from enjoying heaven's beauty.

As human beings, how can we liberate ourselves of all of these worldly chains and help the soul reach its Creator? There are so many spiritual practices our early fathers went through, and with the grace of God they achieved their aim. They recorded their experiences throughout their lives, not over a few days like Jonah's plant, until they were able to obtain the Heavenly Kingdom. The grace of God was active in their spirits, so they could achieve salvation. That is why they are called 'saints,' because they are sanctified by Him and their souls are united with His Holiness. The godliness, righteousness, and purity of their lives flowed over others. They are role models in their silence and quietness as they live away from people, yet remain close to them through their teachings and guidance.

Thus the purity of the soul and heart away from the old man is the condition for a strong and accepted prayer, and so a person becomes a temple of God. This is the whole point of our earthly struggle and fight for perfection, in order to inherit His heavenly glories. When we taste the sweetness of the Lord, we should not race onto the spiritual path, but also have the grace of discernment, enlightened by the guidance of the fathers and the Lord granting us His blessings. Therefore we should be wise and preserve this in our hearts, just like St Mary, who kept all those matters in her heart and gave glory to the Lord. And so preserve your treasure, lest you lose it because of your tongue.

5 June 1970

"And my speech and my preaching were not with persuasive words of human wisdom, but in demonstration of the Spirit and of power, that your faith should not be in the wisdom of men but in the power of God." (1 Cor 2: 4-5)

Our apostle St Paul explains to us through these words about the work of grace and the strength of the Spirit in any area, topic, service or life of consecration, and many times we complain throughout these times of spiritual lukewarmness, despite all the sermons and the continual increase in services which are excellent in knowledge and action. This is also true in monasticism, it did not happen a century ago that you would go to a monastery and find so many intellectually knowledgeable monks residing in there, and yet we repeat what St Arsanius said: "the alphabet that a non-educated person knows, he has not learnt it after Arsanius the teacher of the kings' children".

Thus, in the previous verse, St Paul teaches us that the spiritual life in any place or type of consecration, if it is built on human knowledge and wisdom, then it is weak and has little fruit. However, if it was in demonstration of the Spirit and of the power of God, coming forth from a heart full of faith, hope and deep love, then our building will be rock solid and will not be shaken by temptations and pains, but it will increase the strength of its foundation, and will shine with its deep qualities. This type will grow and spread spiritually in quietness and serenity, away from noise or confusion.

However, a soul that is used to feeding on words and discussions, arguments and many teachings, which St Paul mentions regarding the persuasive words of human wisdom, we see that it will often stop along the path, leaning on a weak staff, "for the kingdom of God is not in word but in power" (1 Cor 4: 20). This explains to us the struggle of our early forefathers, whether they are bishops, martyrs

138

or monks, and how they truly were great in their lives, because it sprang forth from a heart full of grace, and so they struggled and conquered, and reached their destination in deep humility. May our Lord give us of their spirit.

20 July 1970

"For we do not preach ourselves, but Christ Jesus the Lord, and ourselves your bondservants for Jesus' sake" (2 Cor 4:5).

How wonderful is St Paul, the great teacher of the universe, apostle of Jesus Christ, chosen by God. He was a true, faithful, humble person, with a pure heart full of heavenly grace as he writes, "who has shone in our hearts to give the light of the knowledge of the glory of God" (2 Cor.4:6). The words "and ourselves your bondservants" highlight the path of humility for the servant, for while he is of the highest rank in the church as an apostle of Jesus Christ, chosen by God to preach His holy name amongst the nations, he denies himself, which is a problem that often becomes a stumbling block to many servants. St Paul did not introduce himself, to those he was to serve, as a distinguished admirable person but rather as their slave; in another verse he says, "Who then is Paul, and who is Apollos?"

How beautiful is the virtue of humility, for it is praised by all the saints. It has the cloak of divinity worn by the Lord Jesus when He was incarnated and took the form of a slave, without which humanity would not have been introduced to, and blessed by the presence of the Lord Jesus Christ. Let everyone who is permitted by heavenly providence to enter the priesthood consider himself a servant and a slave to his brethren, as is said by the Lord of lords and head of Principalities, "For who is greater, he who sits at the table, or he who serves? Is it not he who sits at the table? Yet I am among you as the One who serves" (Luke 22:27).

May the Lord have mercy on His priests and congregation, and enlighten everyone's heart to know the meaning of service. How sublime is its honour, and how great is its reward. When a servant is called by God and not by people, may he be crowned with the crown of humility, for humility is a grace granted to complete all virtues and is also the basis for carrying on all virtues. We ask this through the intercessions of St Mary and all the saints. Amen.

26 July 1970

Hardened Hearts

"He has blinded their eyes and hardened their hearts, lest they should see with their eyes, lest they should understand with their hearts and turn, so that I should heal them" (John 12:40). This is the prophecy of Isaiah the Prophet, and although it is spoken about those who did not believe in the Lord Jesus Christ, it still applies today with the children of God and the believers. It is seen when the truth is very clear, yet the person in front of you does not want to be convinced, even if everyone else is trying to convince them. That is why, just before this verse, the Lord of Glory says, "walk while you have the light, lest darkness overtake you; he who walks in darkness does not know where he is going" (John 12:35). Here, we see the meaning of having our eyes blinded. May the Lord protect us from this and make us live, and walk in unity with His light, for He is the Light that shines on everyone in the world.

The Prophet also refers to the hardness of the heart of a person who is not living and following the truth, for the heart is the greatest guide to the way of life. We often hear how hard the saints work to plough the ground of their hearts in order to hear the voice of God, so He becomes their guide and light, lighting their way to the correct path leading to eternal life (John 6:45).

Blessed are the eyes that can recognise the correct path. Blessed are the pure hearts that feel the truth and God who is all in all, "But blessed are your eyes for they see, and your ears for they hear" (Matt 13:16).

17 August 1971

"No one engaged in warfare entangles himself with the affairs of this life, that he may please him who enlisted him as a soldier.

And also if anyone competes in athletics, he is not crowned unless he competes according to the rules" (2 Tim 2:4,5). Here, our great teacher St Paul teaches us the legacy of struggle, and the successful struggle is the one chosen and decided for us by the Lord. In verse four above, monks learn how our early fathers succeeded and won victory in their spiritual lives. How they gained sublime virtues, and how strong their relationship was with their Lord. They found favour in His eyes; He rejoiced in them and loved them till the end. This is because they abandoned everything in this world with all its pleasures and desires and simply followed Him. They lived in caves, in the wilderness, and on mountains, not out of fear or because of failure in life, but so that they could empty their hearts and minds of all worldly things to prepare and consecrate them as a dwelling for the Lord. "For what profit is it to a man if he gains the whole world, and loses his own soul?" (Matt 16:26)

Our teacher St Paul the Apostle teaches us that a soldier equipped with the weapons of faith and prayer, who dedicates his time to prayer and is alert to face spiritual struggle is the one who wins and gains the crown. The one who neglects his spiritual canons and duties, and is careless in following the Lord's commandments and the teachings of the Desert Fathers, resembles a soldier who has thrown his weapons away and slept on the battlefield, giving the enemy a chance to conquer him. "Therefore take up the whole armor of God" (Eph 6:13) and "blessesd are those servants whom the master, when he comes, will find watching" (Luke 12:37).

May the Lord make us, His honest soldiers, deserving of His monastic call and ready for the Kingdom of Heaven through the intercessions of His Blessed Mother and all His saints. Amen.

24 October 1971

Hypocrisy

"And when all the people heard Him, even the tax collectors justified God, having been baptised with the baptism of John. But the Pharisees and lawyers rejected the will of God for themselves, not having been baptised by him" (Luke 7:29,30).

Here "all the people" refers to the general congregation. Usually they are the simple ones who quickly and accept the word of God. To everyone, the tax collectors were viewed as sinners, and the Lord Jesus was blamed for sitting and eating with them. The Pharisee justified himself by claiming that he was not like the tax collector.

Similarly in the spiritual life, the simple are aware of their weaknesses and have a good relationship with God. Particularly in monasticism, those who fill the caves and mountains are those who feel that they know and can do nothing, proving the Lord's words, "My strength is made perfect in weakness." (2 Cor 12:9).

The simple were victorious in their struggle against the enemy and able to conquer them by the blood of the Lamb. As for the Pharisees and those who blindly followed the Mosaic law, they rejected the Lord's words and depended on their own knowledge and abilities. They were the ones saying, "With our tongue we will prevail; our lips are our own" (Ps 12:4) They are the ones who cared about the cleanness of the cup and the whitewashing of the tomb from the outside, depending on their own knowledge and keeping Moses' law. They are the ones whom Jesus rebuked for their hard-hearted ways, saying, "Woe to you."

Let us remain aware, lest we only keep the commandments on the surface. Let us dig deeper and ensure that we are building on rock so that our building is strong and steadfast, avoiding potentially ruining that great house. As it says in the Scriptures "and the ruin of that house was great" (Luke 6:49).

May the Lord have mercy on us, and crown our struggle peacefully. We ask this through the intercession of the Mother of God and all the saints. Amen

18 December 1971

Having Faith

"For by faith you stand" (2 Cor 1:24).

A monk cannot bear the hardships of monastic life unless he is strong in his faith in the Lord Jesus Christ. Christ supports and helps him, just as He saved the three young men from the fiery furnace. He also saved Daniel from the lions' den; He preserved Joseph's chastity, and cured Job of all his calamities. A monk should also have faith in the monastic path, believing that this is his style of life to the end. He who repents cannot live a life of worry and doubt at the same time, "in returning and rest you shall be saved; in quietness and confidence shall be your strength." (Isaiah 30:15)… "The Lord is my portion, says my soul" (Lam 3:24). A monk should sincerely believe that all his toils for the love of God is not in vain, "Therefore the LORD will wait, that He may be… For the LORD is a God of justice; Blessed are all those who wait for Him" (Isaiah 30: 18). Also, as St Paul says: "But the Lord is faithful, who will establish you and guard you from the evil one" (2 Thess 3:3-4).

Life in the monastery strengthens faith, through steady prayers, repentance, and following the commandments. This is the life of a monk when he is ordained and the funeral prayer is prayed on him. A dead person does not desire a certain position in the world, nor inside the monastery.

He who really feels that he is dead considers himself last, thus he tolerates insults and humiliation. He never yearns to be the leader over his brethren, but only gives guidance if someone comes for a word of comfort or advice, "Bear one another's burdens, and so fulfill the law of Christ" (Gal 6:2). No power in the whole world can shake the life of such a monk who meets the Lord Jesus and intimately interacts with Him for years, awaiting the release of his soul from his body to be with his beloved, and from here (the monastery) he takes his crown.

4 February 1972

Repentance

"Your sun shall no longer go down, nor shall your moon withdraw itself; for the Lord will be your everlasting light, and the days of your mourning shall be ended" (Isaiah 60:20).

"And the days of your mourning shall be ended" may mean the acceptance of your repentance. As monasticism is a life of repentance, a monk spends his life in prayer, worship, and humility until the grace of God shines within him and he feels the work of the Holy Spirit that comforts and calms him. Therefore he loses interest in worldly desires. Finally, his mind will be occupied with only heavenly matters. Purity of heart is the source of it all, for the heart becomes the dwelling place for God. These are the fruits of the Spirit, a sign of the monk's spiritual maturity is when he reaps the fruits after having worked hard planting and watering, "He who continually goes forth weeping, Bearing seed for sowing, shall doubtless come again with rejoicing, bringing his sheaves with him" (Ps 126:6).

15 March 1972

The Wilderness

"I will even make a road in the wilderness and rivers in the desert. The beast of the field will honor Me, the jackals and the ostriches, because I give waters in the wilderness and rivers in the desert, to give drink to My people, My chosen. This people I have formed for Myself; they shall declare My praise" (Is 43:19-21).

Isn't this a prophecy about monasticism, and the worshippers in the mountains, wilderness and deserts? When he says, "rivers in the desert," this refers to the souls who deserted the world and came to the desert to be filled with the waters of grace and of the Holy Spirit, as our Lord says, "If anyone thirsts, let him come to Me and drink" (John 7:37). The words, "the beast of the field will honour Me, the jackals and the ostriches," is also a reflection of monasticism, which includes people with all sorts of different characters and habits. For example, St Moses the Black, who was a person with wild habits

144

and fierce characteristics, repented and became a great saint. There is many other examples.

When monks live in the wilderness, practice repentance, and obtain humility, they become full of virtue and merits, like streams of spiritual teaching and deep experience. Out of the wilderness came many great teachers and leaders who blessed the entire world and preserved the faith. This is the meaning of the divinely inspired words, "My people, My chosen."

20 March 1972

Spiritual Growth

"Therefore, laying aside all malice, all deceit, hypocrisy, envy and all evil speaking" (1 Peter 2:1,2).

Herein lies the secret of the work of the Holy Spirit and His power in the saints. Being monks or elders who have spent many years in monasticism means nothing to the progress of our spiritual life unless we strive to plant these virtues within ourselves, "laying aside all malice, all deceit, hypocrisy, envy and all evil speaking." If these things do exist, then this is proof of being spiritual immature. We all know that an infant's food is milk; the mind is also nourished only by the pure grace of God, in which there is no evil at all, because "unless you are converted and become as little children, you will by no means enter the kingdom of heaven" (Matt 18:3).

This is the condition for growing and becoming united with God. From this point, we can easily discover how monks may deviate from the right path. We sometimes consider that practicing superficial fasting and prayer in monasticism is sufficient, and that we can keep rotten bones hidden in whitewashed tombs. We need to humble ourselves and sit at the feet of our Saviour, for He is the only one who can raise the dead with a single word, and lift us out of our sin and weakness. He is the one who can give us grace, power and spiritual growth if He sees our great yearning for His blessings, as it is said in the psalm: "May He grant you according to your heart's desire" (Ps 20:4). This is what the saints have struggled with daily, keeping their hearts pure, "Blessed are the pure in heart, for they shall see God" (Matt 5:8).

3 August 1972

Knowing your Calling

"But also for this very reason, giving all diligence, add to your faith virtue, to virtue knowledge, to knowledge self-control… Therefore, brethren, be even more diligent to make your call and election sure, for if you do these things you will never stumble" (2 Peter 1:5,6,10).

How wonderful it is for a person to complete his call, steadfast to the end. Every calling has its struggle, but mixing two paths is wrong, St Isaac the Syrian said: "If you are a layman, live as one, and if you are a monk live as a solitary, but if you try to live both lives you will fail." Also St Peter the Apostle says, "Therefore, brethren, be even more diligent to make your call and election sure" (2 Peter 1:10). As the devil knows that you will gain fruits because of steadfastness, he will keep distracting your thoughts and trying to pull you out of the monastery to fulfill his destructive aim.

St Peter finishes the verse saying, "for if you do these things you will never stumble." Remaining steady and firm in your principles as a monk means you will obtain great protection against sin and failure, thus St Peter orders us to be "diligent." This is not an easy thing; it takes struggle, persistence and hard work. Therefore, do not live at ease and give your soul the chance to choose. The path of the Lord is a straightforward one; may the Lord make us steadfast in fulfilling our call.

9 August 1972

Divine Plan

"then hear in heaven Your dwelling place, and forgive, and act, and give to everyone according to all his ways, whose heart You know, for You alone know the hearts of all the sons of men" (1 Kings 8:39).

This was King Solomon's prayer at the consecration of the temple he built for the Lord. From the verse "give to everyone according to all his ways, whose heart You know," we clearly see that God looks at the heart. With all the good and bad things happening to people around us, we simply put our hands to our lips and repeat with David the Prophet, "I was mute, I did not open my mouth, because it was You Who did it" (Ps 39:9).

God tests the heart and knows what is hidden deep inside. He gives to each person according to his heart's wish, "May He grant you according to your heart's desire" (Ps 20:4). We also call Him 'the Almighty' as He knows our individual conditions and the desires of our hearts, whether good or bad, as well as our inner thoughts. We often wonder at certain situations that we see, which according to our human estimation are unacceptable, and yet we forget that everything is done with sublime wisdom and divine purpose. If we reflect back after the event, we find out that whatever happened was for the best. Let us give glory to our great God who gives everyone his heart's desire. Let us give our lives into His hands in faith, depending totally on Him, and submitting all our worries and sufferings to Him, for He wants only the best for us. Glory be to Him forever.

11 August 1972

The Narrow Gate

"Enter by the narrow gate; for wide is the gate and broad is the way that leads to destruction, and there are many who go in by it. Because narrow is the gate and difficult is the way which leads to life, and there are few who find it" (Matt 7:13,14).

This is the Lord's order and the constitution of the Christian life in general. Belief in the Lord Jesus Christ and our hope of enjoying eternal life mean it is essential to enter by the narrow gate. This gate means carrying the cross daily, as our Lord says that we will face tribulations in this world. We face tribulations because we are fulfilling His commandments. Thus, there is always a struggle between the will of goodness and the power of evil. The gate of desire, enjoyment, evil, hypocrisy, pride, deceit, etc. is wide; anyone can get through it. Few, though, will enter by the narrow gate, which leads to eternity, and they find it only through digging, searching and hardship, "the kingdom of heaven suffers violence, and the violent take it by force" (Matt 11:12).

If this is the case for the Christian laymen, what about the monks who have died to the world, with all its desires and ranks? Hence nowadays there are many calamities and there is much confusion on the correct monastic life, an ideal monk is regarded by people according to his achievement in service and honour in the church. People do not know that all of these things are just weeds. The true fruits of the Spirit that St Paul described are acquired via an austere life, as practiced in the wilderness, deserts and caves by our early fathers.

Monks who struggle to take off the old man to gain these fruits are viewed with dismay by others. People claim they are a failure, as if they are introducing a new form of monasticism by entering by the narrow gate! As monks we need to know that service is very easy, but monasticism is very hard. We honour the servants chosen by God for a certain service, but service for a monk that includes outside ambitions has no spiritual depth at all. True monasticism means reaching spiritual depths that a layman cannot reach; the same applies to a monk serving in the world. So from this point, we understand the philosophy of genuine monastic life in the wilderness and deserts, for its aim and its struggle is digging and searching for the narrow gate.

This is why our Lord Jesus Christ says that few will find Him. We notice that nowadays few are joining the monastic movement, and even fewer monks are searching for the narrow gate. May our Lord grant us perfection and steadfastness to reach the narrow gate, for without Him and His grace we can do nothing.

19 August 1972

Self Love

"For men will be lovers of themselves...traitors, headstrong, haughty, lovers of pleasure rather than lovers of God, having the form of godliness but denying its power" (2 Tim: 3:2;4-5).

What a harsh saying, especially if it is about those who have consecrated their lives for the Lord. I am so afraid that this is a description of me as a monk.

There are many kinds of self love, which are clear to the person himself and to those surrounding him. But sometimes a person may be deceived, and the only thing that helps us to avoid loving ourselves and to follow the Lord's commandment is humility, "If anyone desires to come after Me, let him deny himself, and take up his cross, and follow Me" (Matt 16:24) . A truly humble person is a person who loves God, denies himself, and rejects all desires, the greatest of which is seeking authority.

This is a very dangerous disease, as explained by our early fathers the saints. They related to us how they reached the height of spirituality when they conquered all weakness rooted within the human soul. Human judgment is usually different to God's, because people look at the eyes while the Lord looks at the heart.

When reading the lives of the saints we see their total self denial. This is not an easy thing to achieve, for to live as an earthly angel requires great humility, caring for nothing in this life except pleasing the Lord and following His commandments.

22 August 1972

Self Denial

"Assuredly, I say to you, unless you are converted and become as little children, you will by no means enter the kingdom of heaven. Therefore whoever humbles himself as this little child is the greatest in the kingdom of heaven" (Matt 18:3-4).

We are living in an age of competition where everyone is competing to become the first, the best, or the greatest. But where is the self denial recommended by our Lord?

The more a person humbles himself, the higher he is in virtue. When St Moses the Black asked St Zachariah, "Who is the monk?" the latter took off his monastic hood, which denotes honour in monasticism, and put it under his feet, saying "If a monk is not like this, he cannot become a monk."

Many great saints escaped honour by pretending they were fools or insane, so that they would not fall into vainglory. Now it is the opposite. A monk wants to be a teacher before becoming a disciple. Although everyone admires the idea of self denial and humility, when it comes into practice through tribulations we see the opposite.

We need to be watchful, to concentrate on the Lord's words, "unless you are converted and become as little children, you will by no means enter the kingdom of heaven." The Lord is the one who preserves children. May He grant us His Grace.

24 August 1972

True Wisdom

"Let no one deceive himself. If anyone among you seems to be wise in this age, let him become a fool that he may become wise. For the wisdom of this world is foolishness with God. For it is written, 'He catches the wise in their own craftiness'" (1 Cor 3:18-19).

We have received God's Spirit so that we might know the things given to us by God and to preach them, for we are being taught by the Holy Spirit. "These things we also speak, not in words which man's wisdom teaches but which the Holy Spirit teaches, comparing spiritual things with spiritual. But the natural man does not receive the things of the Spirit of God, for they are foolishness to him; nor can he know them, because they are spiritually discerned. But he who is spiritual judges all things, yet he himself is rightly judged by no one" (1 Cor 2:13-15).

How wonderful are these verses, in which St Paul the teacher and philosopher expresses the work of the Holy Spirit in the soul. He considers the wisdom of this world as foolishness when compared to the Spirit of God dwelling within His saints. Based on this spiritual measurement, the prophets of the Old Testament prophesied and the apostles in the New Testament preached salvation and spread its message throughout the entire world (Rom 10:18). Our saintly fathers lived in the wilderness and deserts with this same Spirit and the world did not deserve even their footsteps. Many philosophers and scientists approached them and sat at their feet to quench their thirst for spirituality through the heavenly wisdom given to them by the Lord of wisdom: "These things we also speak, not in words which man's wisdom teaches but which the Holy Spirit teaches." There is only One true teacher as our Lord says, "But the Helper, the Holy Spirit, whom the Father will send in My name, He will teach you all things, and bring to your remembrance all things that I said to you" (John 14:26).

So how can we acquire the work of the Holy Spirit within ourselves in this spiritually feeble era, when the world is prevailing with all its desires and lust? The only remedy is to go back and meditate deeply and seriously on the lives of our early fathers, the saints, who found favour with their God. He poured His grace on them as they sought Him with all their hearts, expelling all of the idols of lust from their hearts. The Lord is honest in His promises. He gives generously and freely to the ones who seek Him earnestly and those who never look back as Lot's wife did. There in the silence and serenity of the wilderness, where the monks renounce all worldly desires and are united with their Creator, the grace of God works within hundreds and thousands of humble monks. They empty their hearts from all vanity, so they are ready to be filled by the Lord.

3 March 1973

The Way of the Fathers

"…but imitate those who through faith and patience inherit the promises" (Heb 6:12).

Everyone is searching and looking for ways to reach God; one person prefers fasting and asceticism, another prefers staying up all night and being poor by choice, another chooses chastity, while another is very active in his service, and so on.

While I am the least of them, I say in my simplicity that there is nothing better than clinging to the Lord. Mary, who was praised by the Lord, simply sat at His Feet, listening to His words and looking at His face, in order to be united with Him. Her silence and meditation is the greatest proof of her love for the Lord Jesus Christ, glory be to Him.

The sinful woman who bathed His feet with perfume was forgiven all her sins because she loved Him so much. This act of love is also a result of clinging to the Lord. When I say clinging to the Lord, I do not mean we should neglect the struggle to acquire different virtues, but we cannot concentrate totally on them, as if they are the aim in our spiritual life. They are simply a means of helping us to draw closer and closer to abiding in the love of the Lord. When He sees our patience in knocking at His door, He will never let us down. He may take time to test our faith in His love, then when He is sure of our faithfulness and honesty, He will pour the streams of His great love on us.

We are only dust, yet out of His love for us, God purifies us with His grace and dwells within us, filling our hearts with His love and our tongues with His praise. Thus, all our deeds will be from Him and through Him, "for without Me you can do nothing" (John 15:5).

How can we gain the Lord if we are not clinging to Him, waiting for His work in us? This is our hope as it was the hope of our early Desert Fathers, who lived in caves in the wilderness and in monasteries.

May their blessings be with us all. Amen.

6 April 1973

Being Led by the Spirit

'For as many as are led by the Spirit of God, these are sons of God" (Rom 8:14).

This is the trademark of a successful person; checking ourselves before condemning others. Am I a person led by the Spirit of God? Do I give the grace of God a chance to work in me and through me so that I can see His great deeds in my weak self? Do I follow St Mary's example of keeping everything in her heart? Do I depend on my personal experiences and education and plan for every occasion?

Here, the cunning devil interferes with all my deeds to distract me from following the Lord Christ and from His grace within me. Finally, I discover the bitter fact; all the things I have achieved have collapsed because they were built on sand, depending on myself. I did not yield to the grace of God, nor seek guidance from the pious men of God in humility. This is seen very clearly in the life of worship and monasticism. We have never heard, and will never hear, of any monk who made spiritual progress or acquired any grace as a result of his human power. We are not ignoring the various struggles and wars in the monastic path, however they are useless if they are not supported by the grace of God. It is exactly like the work of fire in coal, or the need for leaves to preserve the fruit of the trees.

Nothing is more beautiful and joyful for a monk than to wait for the work of grace of God within him, no matter how long it takes. All of the fights, struggles, and wars with the devils that a monk faces are part of the life of submission. He has given his life as a sacrifice of love to the Lord Jesus Christ. Thus, he is truly led by the Spirit of God, and deserves to be called a son of God. How great is this sonship and honourable title to the poor humble monk, who becomes one of God's special sons, ready to inherit the Kingdom,

"For as many as are led by the Spirit of God, these are sons of God."

16 July 1973

"Then Jesus said to them, "Do not be afraid. Go and tell My brethren to go to Galilee, and there they will see Me." (Matt 28: 10)

"Then the eleven disciples went away into Galilee, to the mountain which Jesus had appointed for them…but some doubted." (Matt 28: 16-17)

This is the commandment of the Lord, that whoever seeks to see Him, he must go to Galilee, where He is visibly seen. On the mountain, the fog of worries and various sins will be lifted from our hearts. The monastic fathers teach us how to purify our hearts, as they obtained the purity of heart on mountains and in lives spent in deserts; lives of quietness and tranquility in monastires, where they experienced the verse "Blessed are the pure in heart, for they shall see God". The disciples went to the mountain where the Lord ordered them to go, "When they saw Him, they worshiped Him; but some doubted." These words have strong connotations, and they show its powerful effect over the years and centuries until this day. Those who worship God, they worship Him in Spirit and truth, but whoever doubts will never reach his goal, and his love will never be complete. Many have come to this life of monasticism, and when time passed, and they could not see Christ, and they kept waiting to see the revelation, and when they still could not see it, they went back. It was the cloud of temptation and various other struggles, which was supposed to accompany them to see Christ, has made them doubt in the reliability of the revelation; they did not know that 'with your patience you will possess your soul.'

However, those who worshiped Jesus, did so out of submission to His will, and in want of fulfilling His commandment, and bearing everything set in their path. Whether they see the revelation or not, or whether their eyes are capable of seeing or they have been dirtied, their concern is still to fulfil the commandments of the Lord, "…to go to Galilee, and there they will see Me."

This is our faith in our Lord Jesus Christ, that He is honest and just in fulfilling His promises. Whoever looks upon Him, his face will shine and be enlightened, and will not be ashamed. Steadfastness in the calling of the Lord is evident for us, and this in itself is a revelation coming out of a strong faith in Christ. However hard it may be to go up the mountain, it will inevitably bring a monk who rejoices in the calling of the Lord, to receive a pure heart, and thus be able to see Him.

However, whoever doubts, and goes back, then the enemy will receive him and drown him in the waves of this world. He will not know where he is going because darkness has covered his eyes, and fear has defeated him. For this reason, the Lord says to His children, "Do not fear."

Truly, when they saw Him, they worshipped Him, but some doubted. May the Lord make us worthy to be true worshippers in Spirit and truth, hating the lusts of the world and its glory, and my soul shall chant 'The LORD is my portion, therefore I hope in Him!

10 February 1974

"And my speech and my preaching were not with persuasive words of human wisdom, but in demonstration of the Spirit and of power, that your faith should not be in the wisdom of men but in the power of God." (1 Cor 2: 4-5)

We know that the power of the Christian faith is not in the influence of words or earthly wisdom, but through the power of the Holy Spirit, and His work in the non-believer. For this reason, it was very difficult to preach to pagan worshippers, and non Christians. True and successful service is not words in sermons, as much as it is the work of the Holy Spirit in the servant and in the listener. For the Spirit must go forth and prepare the ears to listen to accept the word of God.

29 April 1974